TRACING YOUR FREEMASON, FRIENDLY SOCIETY AND TRADE UNION ANCESTORS

TRACING YOUR FREEMASON, FRIENDLY SOCIETY AND TRADE UNION ANCESTORS

A Guide for Family Historians

Daniel Weinbren

Pen & Sword
FAMILY HISTORY

First published in Great Britain in 2019
PEN & SWORD FAMILY HISTORY
an imprint of
Pen & Sword Books Ltd
47 Church Street, Barnsley, South Yorkshire, S70 2AS

Copyright © Daniel Weinbren, 2019

ISBN 978 1 52671 033 8

The right of Daniel Weinbren to be identified as Author of the Work has been asserted by him in accordance with the Copyright, Designs and Patents Act 1988.

A CIP catalogue record for this book is available from the British Library.

All rights reserved. No part of this book may be reproduced or transmitted in any form or by any means, electronic or mechanical including photocopying, recording or by any information storage and retrieval system, without permission from the Publisher in writing.

Typeset in Palatino and Optima by CHIC GRAPHICS

Printed and bound in England by TJ International Ltd, Padstow, Cornwall

Pen & Sword Books Ltd incorporates the imprints of Pen & Sword Airworld, Archaeology, Atlas, Aviation, Battleground, Discovery, Family History, Fiction, History, Maritime, Military, Military Classics, Politics, Select, Social History, True Crime, Frontline Books, Leo Cooper, Remember When, Seaforth Publishing, The Praetorian Press, Wharncliffe Local History, Wharncliffe Transport, Wharncliffe True Crime and White Owl.

For a complete list of Pen & Sword titles please contact

PEN & SWORD BOOKS LTD
47 Church Street, Barnsley, South Yorkshire, S70 2AS, England
E-mail: enquiries@pen-and-sword.co.uk
Website: www.pen-and-sword.co.uk
or
PEN & SWORD BOOKS LTD
1950 Lawrence Rd, Havertown, PA 19083, USA
E-mail: Uspen-and-sword@casematepublishers.com
Website: www.penandswordbooks.com

CONTENTS

Preface		vii
Acknowledgements		xi
Chapter 1	**Links and Divisions**	1
	Brotherly Love	1
	Distinctiveness and Blurred Boundaries	4
	Advancement	7
Chapter 2	**Digging Where You Stand**	11
	Material Culture	11
	Personal Testimony	16
Chapter 3	**Press Reports**	24
	Local Stories	24
	Press Bias	28
Chapter 4	**Fraternity Before About 1800**	35
	The Ancient World	35
	Guilds	37
	Drama	39
	The Long Eighteenth Century	44
Chapter 5	**Freemasonry**	48
	Records	53
	Charity	63
	Ornamentation	64
	Social Base	65
	Specialist Lodges	72
	Imperial Connections	78
	Twentieth Century	82

Chapter 6	Friendly Societies	89
	The Long Nineteenth Century	90
	1911: National Insurance	120
	Further Roles for the State	126
Chapter 7	Trade Unions	132
	Since the 1790s	133
	From 1914	144
	Since the 1940s	162
	Sources and Collections	171
	Digging Deeper	178
Bibliography		179
Index		184

PREFACE

For hundreds of years there has been an allure about the notion of, to use Shakespeare's phrase in *Henry V*, a band of brothers. It evokes images of structured fellowship, men fiercely loyal to one another, united for a cause greater than themselves and transforming the communities in which they lived and worked. For centuries fraternal organisations have thrived all over the world, offering variously, opportunities for sociability, moral improvement and friendship. Although there have been many societies for women and for men and women, there have been more open only to men. These may have been attractive because they provided spaces for men to relax together. There have been numerous charitable and sociable fraternal bodies. For information about a wide range of these types of bodies see David Harrison and Fred Lomax, *Freemasonry & fraternal societies* (2015) and Victoria Solt Dennis, *Discovering Friendly and Fraternal Societies: their badges and regalia* (2005). Three types of fraternal organisations, friendly societies, trade unions and Freemasonry, have dominated the field and played significant roles in shaping both legislation and civil society as well as people's understandings of mutual support. This book is focused on those types of bodies. While you may turn first to the chapter on one group of fraternal bodies. You might then consult another part of this book. Members of one fraternal branch may be connected to another. In recent years male leaders of the Ancient Order of Foresters at High Court, their annual meeting, have met there as Freemasons. In a 2001 speech nominating David Philips as Grand Master of one of the major friendly societies, the Oddfellows, it was noted that he was 'a keen ritualist which may stem from his strong masonic connections'. In recent years the Oddfellows has ceased to trade in financial services.

It now aims to be, as a leading officer put it, a 'mutual caring Society, but with an up-to-date twist'. However, it maintains some of its rituals, described by one life-long member as 'a means of explaining to the membership what its fundamental principles are and wrapping that round with some aspects of Freemasonry ritual'. If your ancestor enjoyed associational culture, sociable ritual and collective activity that ancestor may well have joined a union and a friendly society and also have been a Freemason.

In 1921 the Amalgamated Society of Carpenters, Cabinetmakers and Joiners joined with the General Union of Carpenters and Joiners to form the Amalgamated Society of Woodworkers (ASW). These ASW brass badges date from about 1950, when the union was the seventh largest in the country. The one on the left would have been worn by members of the English branches and the badge on the right by members of the Irish branches. In 1971 the ASW merged with other unions to form the Union of Construction, Allied Trades and Technicians (UCATT). (© Stuart Williams)

People who wanted support in times of trouble, such as the illness or death of a breadwinner, often turned to fraternal societies. These were seen as providing a space away from the alienating market place and (in many cases) the feminine domestic sphere. In Britain fraternity has been hugely influential within both the voluntary and the state sectors for hundreds of years. Many fraternal organisations offered conviviality, singing and parades, loyalty oaths, dress codes, graveside duties, drinking, formalised hierarchies, imagined ancestry, passwords and signs and initiation rites, often symbolising a new birth. While there was a wide range of motives for joining, across all bodies there may have been a shared interest in financial security, trade or business contacts and a place to meet like-minded people. This cultural mortar bound together members through a shared sense of obligation, responsibility and purpose. Often health and welfare, including charity, and control over work were central to their versions of fraternalism. Through fraternal bodies people became familiar with ideas of self-government as a supplement to rule by the Church or monarch. They gained experience of reaching decisions (including deciding for themselves who should be the officials) through discussion and votes. They became familiar with making payments to the lodge and sending representatives to national assemblies. Ideas of equality of opportunity were developed within lodges. Members were united by drama and symbolism and could conceptualise themselves as meeting outside the hierarchies of the class structure, the family and the workplace.

The first chapter here includes an outline of the common ancestors of friendly societies, trade unions and Freemasonry. It illuminates their similarities and borrowings from one another. Although Freemasonry retains many of these elements, no longer are members of all those in these bodies obliged to swear oaths or to engage with spiritual values taught through ritual dramas or to use ceremonies, symbols and allegory to promote moral and social virtues and principles of brotherly love, equality and mutual aid. Nevertheless, members of one would often join another fraternal organisation and ideas flowed between them. This is followed by two chapters about important sources. First there are those that might be close to hand, material culture, such as the regalia that an ancestor left behind and personal testimony and the recollections of the reminiscences of others who may have been their brethren. Attention is then paid to press coverage of fraternal bodies, much of which is available online. Chapter 4 is about how these organisations helped their members advance socially as the associations gained more status within the wider society. The focus is on the development of fraternal associations from Roman times until the Napoleonic Wars at the end of the eighteenth century. Although divergent in their aims and activities, the three types of association are all considered in this chapter. The next three chapters are specifically about Freemasonry during the period since the 1790s, friendly societies in that period and then about trade-unionism in the same time span.

ACKNOWLEDGEMENTS

My thanks to the numerous archivists, scholars and librarians who have offered advice and ideas over many years, particularly Simon Fowler. The publishers have been supportive. I am also indebted, as ever, to Rebecca, Miriam, Jacob and Bethany who have, in unequal measure, both taken me away from and encouraged me to engage with writing.

Please note that by the time this book is published websites referred to may have moved. If the links provided in this book fail, then try trying typing key words into a search engine (one of these is Google but there are others) and you may well find the sites that way.

Chapter 1

LINKS AND DIVISIONS

The three types of associational form considered in this book have common ancestors and recognisably similar familial traits. Although friendly societies, unions and Freemasonry have all moved away from the associational form from which they all developed, nevertheless, they are still recognisably siblings. While there have been exceptions, in general they have tended to draw on ideas of masculine collective self-help built upon self-governing and self-funding and bolstered by ritual and public displays. The *Cheshire Observer and General Advertiser* of 13 December 1856 reported the differences between Oddfellows and Freemasons as understood by a man in a pub. 'I didn't mean a mason with a hod of mortar: he'd be a hod fellow, don't you see? – there's a fine old crusted joke for you – I mean a mason with a petticut, a freemason'. This effort at humour indicates that there was a recognition that different fraternal bodies have shared and exchanged ideas and learnt from one another.

BROTHERLY LOVE
This notion of a family is reflected in the language employed. Using the word 'brother' has enabled fraternal bodies to emphasise their similarity to idealised notions of the family, perhaps in order to promote charitable, trusting sentiments and reciprocity. Female friendly societies and unions which permitted both men and women to join often used the term 'sister', but some female Freemasons used 'brother' as a term of address for one another. It also indicated that membership was limited to those who shared goals and values and sometimes affection. Although some unions and friendly

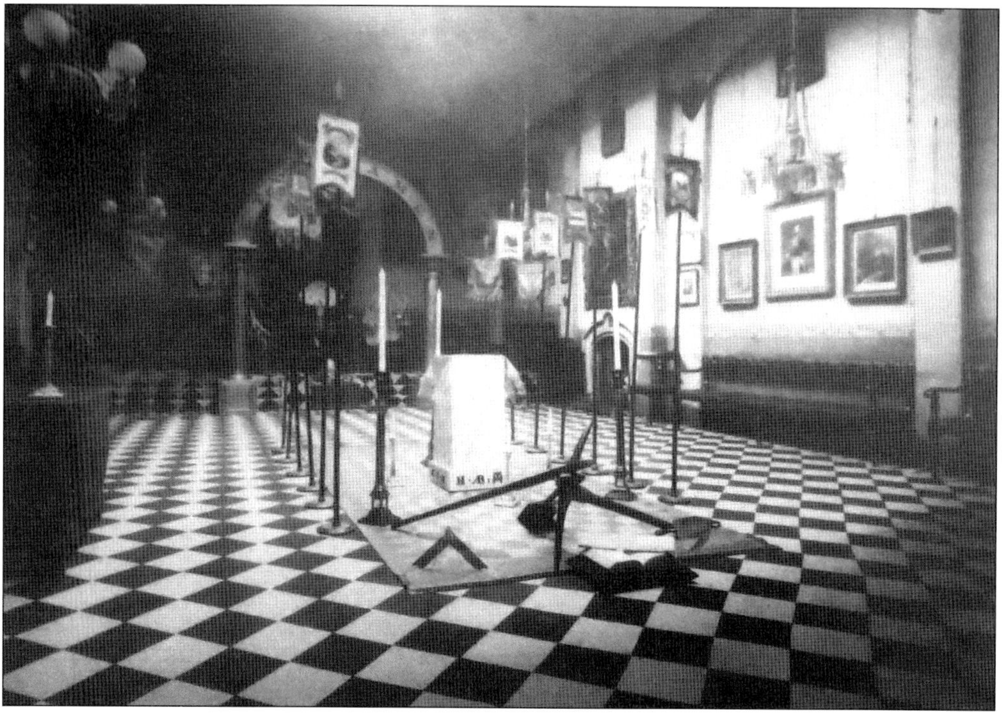

Halford Street Masonic Hall, Leicester, set out for Masonic ceremonies. From Aubrey Newman, David Hughes and Don Peacock, Freemasonry in Leicestershire and Rutland. The 'Other' Orders and degrees, The Provincial Grand Lodge of Leicestershire and Rutland, Leicester (2012).

societies have had specialist aims, being open only to specific gender, social, work-based, ethnic or religious groups, fraternities have tended to promote reflection, toleration, self-improvement and charitable activity. Employing kinship terms, such as brethren and mother lodge, staked a claim to a linage back to the Church (in which monks were brothers and the Pope the Holy Father) and to the notion of kinship between those not related by blood or marriage. When he addressed a friendly society conference in England in 1842, James L. Ridgely of Baltimore referred to the 'members of one great family [. . .] children of one great parent'. This society had branches in the USA and he suggested that American brethren offer prayers 'for the welfare of the Mother'. Union leader Jack Dash called his 1969 autobiography *Good Morning, Brothers!* When researching, look out for the words brother or sister in correspondence to your ancestor. It might well indicate that they were thought to be part of a non-biological family.

By the mid-nineteenth-century there was a tradition of support for travelling brothers be they Masons, or fellow members of friendly societies or unions. Members of specific trades who were paid up members of a fraternal body and who were seeking work could arrive in a town and expect to be offered accommodation for a night and, if there was one, a job. If there was no work they were obliged to move on. The system enabled information to be passed around and potential blacklegs to be dispersed in times of industrial dispute. Through running a similar system, the Oddfellows helped to support the unemployed, regulated the supply of skilled labour and enabled men to travel. However, the Oddfellows had an additional proviso, 'that no member shall be allowed a card who has lost his employ through a strike or turn-out for wages – trades' unions not being countenanced by the Order'. If your ancestor went 'on the road' looking for work, or even looking for adventure on what has been called the 'Poor's Man's Grand Tour', then that might explain how that ancestor reached the town in which they resided, having been born elsewhere.

Brotherly support could also take the form of unity against women. While many guilds accepted women as members, they were excluded from positions of authority and until the twentieth century often women were excluded from many fraternities. Many men argued that women were more curious than men and had an inability to keep secrets. Some also cited biblical support for separating men and women and noted the legal status of women, that many lacked financial independence and that childbirth was a dangerous activity. In cases where women gained greater control over the household and the children, some men saw fraternal organisations as a place of sanctuary and brotherly support. The Druids (a friendly society) claimed links with Moses, who won freedom with the help of his brother. The Foresters (also a friendly society) claimed links with Robin Hood, who led a group of men who strove for greater independence. An important Masonic ritual involves a drama in which a dead man is resurrected and supported by his brethren. Many of the symbols of the Orange Order and its sibling Protestant organisations, the Royal Arch Purple Chapter and the Royal Black Institution, can also be seen as supportive of the notion of heroic men without women. When there were female images they tended be of either virtues, such as the Roman goddess of Justice, or victims, often widows. Do not assume that the strongest bonds your male ancestor had was with his kin by blood or marriage. He might have felt close links with his brothers in the lodge and helped or been helped by lodge members.

DISTINCTIVENESS AND BLURRED BOUNDARIES
Often the boundaries between the different types of fraternity were blurred. In 1800 in Warrington, the Masonic Lodge of Lights had both a Masonic Benefit Society and links to the White Hart Benefit Society. In Bristol the Temple Lodge Benefit Society was both a Masonic Lodge and a friendly society. In 1790, members of the Masonic Lodge of Fidelity, Leeds, established one of the largest friendly societies, now known as the Foresters Friendly Society. In

the early nineteenth century miners in the north east formed the Brotherly Friendly Society, which was also known as the Union of Pitmen. The Manchester weavers' strike of 1808 was sustained by friendly societies. In Wiltshire and Somerset, where there was a federation of shearmen's box clubs, the Home Secretary Spencer Percival noted when Wiltshire shearmen destroyed some gig-mills in 1802: 'it is most probable that they are too cunning to keep any papers but such as would be referable to little more than a friendly society'. It was a frequent complaint of the authorities that friendly societies allowed members to withdraw funds when on strike and in 1812 Macclesfield was said to be 'full of sick and burial societies which are the germ of revolution'. In 1830 a federal Friendly Society of Coal Mining was founded in Bolton. It did not promote mutual aid in the manner of the major friendly societies of the period but instead enjoyed some success as a trade union. It spread from Lancashire to Staffordshire, Wales and Derbyshire but in the face of lock-outs, blacklegging and legal repression, it crumbled in 1831. Regalia could be taken as a sign of fraternity. When in 1830, a period of widespread machine-breaking, John Benett, Tory MP for Wiltshire, met a group of men who wore 'party-coloured sashes' and threatened to destroy his machinery. Benett said: 'I am sorry to see you with that sash on ... Young man, that sash will hang you'. The men went on to destroy Benett's threshing machines while wearing the sashes. When a fraternal association presents itself as law-abiding and respectable you can, as a researcher, be sceptical. At different times Freemasonry, friendly societies and unions have all been deemed to be a threat to the social order.

It was not until 1871 that the term 'trade union' appeared in legislation. Bodies that became unions provided insurance while those which were friendly societies defended workplace communities. Benevolent societies, workingmen's clubs, specially authorised societies, specially authorised loan societies, medical societies and cattle insurance societies, which were all registered as friendly societies under the Friendly Societies Acts. The total membership of these organisations in 1899 was 610,254. The Friendly Iron Moulders' Society was founded in 1809, became the Friendly Society of Operative Iron Moulders of the United Kingdom of Great Britain and Ireland. In 1920 it merged with other bodies to become the National Union of Foundry Workers. The Friendly Society of Operative Stonemasons of England, Ireland and Wales formed in 1833, changed its name to the Operative Society of Masons, Quarrymen and Allied Trades of England and Wales in 1919. Builders' and stonemasons' union records can be found at the Working Class Movement Library, https://www.wcml.org.uk. When you come across an ancestor in a trade union, bear in mind that the organisation may well have had friendly society functions. Some friendly societies operated as unions.

Sometimes the boundaries between fraternal association were made explicit. While some fraternal bodies attracted working men, some were more elitist. Some permitted women and men to join but many were single-sex. Some were long-lived with members across the country and the British Empire and beyond. Masonic membership was an aid to migration to South Africa and elsewhere, with men joining shortly before departure so as to have contacts when they arrived. Freemasonry spread with, and facilitated the work of, the British Empire. Fraternity offered practical, financial and emotional support to those who moved far from their homes. There were cofraternities for Jews and for Jesuits, friendly societies for French Huguenots in London and Germans in Bradford. In Wales the Irish settlers created their own friendly societies which promoted local and national patriotism. The United Irishmen also promoted national identity, the Orange Orders, representing Protestants, were fraternal bodies largely in Ireland and Scotland, the Irish National Foresters was open to men of any religion or class who were 'Irish by birth or descent' while the William the Fourth Society of Deptford, London excluded all Irish people. Members of the Philanthropic Ivorites promoted the Welsh language within a fraternal framework. Your ancestor may have chosen to identify as (for example) Irish or may have been banned from a society on account of his birthplace.

The Freemasons and many trade unions and friendly societies have split into factions. Numerous trade unions amalgamated as needs changed. Sometimes fraternal bodies transformed themselves. The organisations have developed separate functions and aims and have long been regulated by different laws. When looking for a specific trade union note that newspapers, or other accounts, are not always accurate. It is easy to confuse the East End Cabinet Makers' Association with the London Society of Cabinet Makers or the Cabinet Makers' Society. They were not one and the same. You may well have come across name variations in your family tree. This is a problem of a similar order. Many friendly societies and trade unions were small, local and short-lived. Sometimes they merged or split. Within any one trade there could be several unions in any one area and few national unions until the twentieth century. Lodges of all types frequently opened and closed. The more data you can acquire, the narrower your search will be when you come to consult the list of known unions. A helpful site is Trade Union Ancestors, www.unionancestors.co.uk. There is an official list of active trade unions and former trade unions here, https://www.gov.uk/government/publications/public-list-of-active-trade-unions-official-list-and-schedule.

ADVANCEMENT
Membership could lead to personal and collective advancement. Gaining additional 'degrees' through passing tests set by the organisation could build a brother's credit rating and enable him to gain enhanced access to strings which might be pulled. Collectively, ritual and hierarchy helped union members defend the frontiers of what was defined as skilled work. Fraternities could also give members access to official recognition. In 1815, the London-based, men-only guild, the Society of Apothecaries, was licensed by statue to provide a system of education, assessment and registration. A century later some friendly societies and unions were 'approved' to

Freemason Eugene E. Hawkins, 1913–2003, in his Masonic regalia in about 1961. The regalia can be used to identify his lodge and rank within Freemasonry. Perhaps the picture also shows some of the pride that this Mason had in being a 'brother'.

administer National Insurance. Often the law offered only limited protection against defaulters. Payment in kind and credit were endemic to much of the economy. Fraternal organisations which emphasised the importance of honour and civility could help merchants to build trust with one another, and could help trade-unionists to build solidarity required to ensure a pay rise. It was often within the fraternal association that members learnt how to interact on a formal basis. The concepts of business ethics and polite society developed symbiotically with fraternal organisations. This included both the friendly societies, which dominated the burials insurance market, and the Freemasons. The 1867 extension of the franchise to many working men was secured in part because high friendly society membership was seen as evidence that working men were able to demonstrate good citizenship. In recognition of the training that fraternal associations could provide one of the first Labour MPs explained in 1906 that he had 'graduated in the university of the friendly societies'.

DISPLAY
Parades were a means by which fraternal organisations advertised their presence and their activities. Late medieval York, for example, had a plethora of crafts fraternities and guilds which provided mutual support and promoted religious processions. There are many examples of such spectacles during the period since then. The parade to mark the opening of the Derby Arboretum in central England in 1840 was led by the town councillors. They were followed by fraternal organisations in strict hierarchical order. All the societies had at least one banner and the larger societies boasted several. During a Royal visit to Lewes the crowds were policed by officers of fraternal organisations. Freemasons tend not to march in the streets today, but they did until the 1930s. Trade unions still demonstrate and a number of local friendly societies continue to hold annual parades in the villages in which they are based.

Freemasonry, friendly societies and trade unions are separate to one another. Their activities, structures and funding have changed over time. However, there are some elements common to all three types of fraternal body. They offered opportunities for often-male-dominated drama, rituals and bonding through shared social activities. Although some friendly societies had patrons, and some unions had a significant degree of control by employers, fraternal organisations tend to be largely self-governing and self-funding, treating their members as capable of exercising responsibility and preparing members to take on the challenges of leadership and self-organisation. You might find that your ancestor was in more than one type of fraternity and that his, or her, reasons for joining and remaining a member might have been similar whether it was a trade union or a Masonic lodge.

Chapter 2

DIGGING WHERE YOU STAND

Before picking up this specialist book you will have probably have visited one of the many generic online guides such as https://www.genguide.co.uk. You may have studied a free online course such as this one at: https://www.futurelearn.com/ courses/genealogy. There is a useful free Open University short video about how historians find out about the past at: http://www. open.edu/openlearn/history-the-arts/history/how-do-historians-know-about-the-past?in_menu=713874&utm_source=Twitter&utm_medium=social&utm_campaign=SocialSignIn.

As well as looking online, an early step to take in your investigations is, if possible, to look for physical material about your ancestor who was in a fraternal body. Here you might find clues as to which union they were in, how many years they were a Freemason or if they held a rank or formal position within the specific friendly society they joined. This chapter is about the objects and also memories left by your ancestor.

MATERIAL CULTURE
Wills often included a list of instructions as to how the possessions of the deceased should be distributed. About 6 per cent of those who died in England and Wales at the end of the eighteenth century left wills and about 10 per cent by 1841. Although many wills had general phrases covering movable property such as 'household goods, furniture utensils' or sometimes 'pictures, wine or liquor', on occasion specific items were mentioned. Wills might mention

Masonic glassware or a watch fob. Some wills also mention specific instructions regarding the memorials or headstones. Obituaries of Freemasons often mention a Masonic charity. Although a tombstone engraved with a square and compasses does not guarantee that your ancestor was a Freemason (such symbols were used by others), it is a sign that the deceased was probably a member of a fraternal body. Other material culture that you might find in the personal possession of a member of a fraternal organisation includes postcards and copies of *Foresters' Miscellany* or *Odd Fellows Magazine* or other periodicals. It is sometimes possible to identify individuals from their regalia. For example, often sashes would have initials on them denoting the rank of the wearer.

If you find a membership card such as this, you can tell which Court (branch) of the Ancient Order of Foresters Friendly Society that labourer James Reeve joined, when he joined and who witnessed that James was in good bodily health. (Private collection)

This membership certificate is displayed in a pub, the Foresters Arms, Graffham. George Albery was born and bred in this Sussex village. He rose to become High Court Ranger, that is the elected head of the whole, vast society. It is likely that an Ancient Order of Foresters Friendly Society Court met in this pub. (© foresterssussex)

Once you have gathered all the artefacts, the membership card, the newspaper clipping, then try to check the stories. Bear in mind that societies and unions split and merge. Some Masonic lodges changed names and meeting places but retained links to the same town. In Sunderland the Sea Captains' Lodge No. 218, formed on 14 January 1757, metamorphosed into The Palatine Lodge No. 97. Other lodges associated with regiments travelled when their members moved. Finding out when and where lodges met is facilitated by searching the electronic version of the printed volume, John Lane's *Masonic Records 1717–1894*. There is more about this in Chapter 5. An individual might be a Freemason, a trade-unionist and a member of a friendly society – all at the same time. Many people confuse Oddfellows and Freemasons. You might be told that somebody was an Oddfellow but note that there have been numerous bodies calling themselves Oddfellows. These include, for example, the Nottingham Imperial Oddfellows and the Independent Order of Oddfellows (Manchester Unity). The latter was far more popular and in this book all references to the Oddfellows refer to the IOOF (MU) unless otherwise stated. The regalia might lead you to conclude that the ancestor was a Freemason, but plenty of other bodies have similar regalia and traditions. The Royal Antediluvian Order of Buffaloes, founded in 1822, is largely a charitable and sociable body with rituals and titles which echo those of the Freemasons. The Grand Order of Water Rats is an entertainment industry fraternity which supports charities, many within the performing industries. Formed in 1869, it has titles (such as Prince Rat) and jewels (medals) and a motto which reflects similar values to other fraternities, 'Philanthropy, conviviality and social intercourse'. The International Order of Good Templars also uses ritual and regalia which are similar to the Freemasons. It, however, admits men and women and it promotes temperance. The Orange Order, an international Protestant fraternity, also has a structure which is likely to have drawn on friendly societies or the Freemasons, see http://www.grandorangelodge.co.uk. There are many other such bodies.

You can sometimes identify the items that belonged to your fraternal ancestor from guidebooks. Victoria Solt Dennis' *Discovering Friendly and Fraternal Societies* (2005) is recommended. Keith

Jackson's *Beyond the Craft: The Indispensable Guide to Masonic Orders Practised in England and Wales* (6th edn, 2012) is one of several guides to the regalia associated with additional Masonic degrees, such as the Knights Templar. W. Kirk Macnulty's *Freemasonry, symbols, secrets, significance* (2006), has 386 illustrations, 327 of them in colour and also contains a list of some of the Masonic museums and libraries of the world. Written by a Freemason, it includes suggested reading and information about other resources. Help with identification can sometimes be found in local and specialist fraternal archives or museums such as The Kent Museum of Freemasonry, in St Peter's Place, Canterbury, Kent, http://kent museumoffree masonry.org.uk, and the Warrington Museum of Freemasonry at Warrington Masonic Hall, Winmarleigh House, 15, Winmarleigh Street, Warrington, http://museum.westlancsfree masons.org.uk.

People may not have told you that an uncle was a member of the Order of the Secret Monitor or a grandfather's belongings included an Ancient Order of Foresters sash simply because you never asked. If your ancestor is not available, it can be useful to listen to appropriate relatives. This recollection of childhood trips to an Oddfellows lodge is from Daniel Weinbren's *The Oddfellows: 200 Years of Making Friends and Helping People* (2010). It reveals something of the world of friendly society rituals as recalled by a person who was not then a member:

> You're not allowed in until you are 16 but I used to peep through the keyhole [of the Oddfellows Hall] when I was allowed to go and sit in the kitchen to see my Dad doing his bit and all the regalia. We used to take the key out very quietly and our respective Dads, both tall, were always given the Conductors job because they looked very efficient and very regal with full regalia and the wands. A thing that you carry in one hand, it's got an open hand in it with a red heart in the middle.

Singing together had a binding effect on the members of fraternal bodies and the lyrics reminded them of the ideals of their organisation. These items were produced by a friendly society but you may well find songbooks for unions and Freemasons among the possessions of your ancestor. (Author's collection)

PERSONAL TESTIMONY

Below are some ideas about gathering evidence by recording people. These apply whether the person is a relative or not.

- Try to maximise the value of the contribution of informants by asking detailed questions about direct experience.
- Treat all interviewees with respect and courtesy by abiding by their preferences as to the location and conduct of the interview.
- Be clear to the interviewee as to the purpose of the interview and its possible uses.
- Be sure to have done sufficient research in advance.

- Be sure to have sufficient technical knowledge. Have a practice interview in advance.
- When you record you can have one eye on future scholarship and on making the recording available to others.
- You should also make it clear to the interviewee that while they control who can access the recording, that you would like the copyright to rest with a suitable archive. To do this you should get the signed, informed consent of the interviewee.
- Seek out advice on best practices and rights from the Oral History Society website.
- Ensure that, if you have offered a copy of the recording to the interviewee, a copy is supplied.
- After the recording, when you express thanks (in writing if possible) try to reiterate the purposes and value of the recording.

If there is somebody to interview, then, in advance, do a bit of research and prepare a list of questions. You need not ask all of them, but they will jog your memory during the interview and allow you to listen, rather than worry about the next question. People's memories are likely to include opinions and recollections of half-forgotten events and fascinating, sometimes well-rehearsed, tales. Most of us get the dates wrong or telescope two events into one account. Ask people specific questions about their direct experiences. Even if you want to know about a relative's time as a trade-union activist, questions about their earlier life might reveal details of time spent in another union or with an influential trade-union official. If the interviewee describes their job you will get a sense of working relationships. Why they led that strike, or how they stopped a potential walk-out. Moreover, the detail will provide wider context and help you understand why your Uncle Stan joined the United Ancient Order of Druids (not to be confused with the Ancient Order of Druids or the Order of Druids) and remained a member all his life.

People forget and they are not typical, representing only themselves. The poorer, unhealthier and unluckier die younger and only the articulate will step forward. Their accounts will indicate their own interpretations but, nevertheless, they could provide you with fresh information about the past, new insights and better understandings of how they comprehend the world. People often recall one set of events through the prism of other events. It is difficult to disentangle hindsight selection and nostalgia. On the other hand, truth is rarely improved by being as close to an event and, like autobiography or diaries, oral testimony can be valid as one person's account. The interpretation of an individual, their performance of a story, can be seen as evidence about the past. A single interview, a single perspective, can illustrate social and historical developments. Even if you do not manage to record your own ancestor, when you rescue the individual from the crowd you add human context, you recognise the value of individual experience and, if the story is about the friendly society, the testimony can articulate a shared reality about membership. What you hear may be the evaluations, the theories, the self-censorship, the taboos, the silences, the understandings, some of them you might call modern myths, which helped sustain the friendly societies.

Explain to the interviewee what you plan to do with the information they provide. If you record the person it could well be helpful to others if you were to get the written permission of your interviewee as to how the material can be used and then to lodge a copy of your recording in an appropriate archive. Before you dismiss this idea, think how pleased you would be if you came across a recording of one of your ancestors. This is not impossible as there are a huge number of recordings in this country and people have been collecting for decades, certainly since the spread of cheap recording equipment in the 1970s. You can find out more about interviewing, equipment, ethical issues and archives from the Oral History Society's website, http://www.ohs.org.uk.

Fraternal bodies often produced biographical accounts of their leaders, with pictures of these men. These are from the Oddfellows' centenary booklet, produced in 1910 and which also contained details of the anniversary concert. (Author's collection)

There are transcripts and collections of personal testimony in archives and libraries around the country. Some collections include recordings of people active in fraternal bodies before there was recording equipment. For example, Charles Booth organised a vast study of the people of London in the late Victorian era. His *Inquiry into the Life and Labour of the People in London* is a seventeen-volume survey begun in the 1880s (when *Life and Labour of the People* appeared) and concluded in 1903 when the last volume of the third edition was published. It is available online at: https://archive.org/stream/lifeandlabourpe02bootgoog/lifeandlabourpe02bootgoog_djvu.txt. The original notes and data, the interviews, questionnaires, statistical information and observations have been preserved in a collection which is far more extensive than the published material. Much is not available to view online but can be seen by visiting the Reading Room in the British Library of Political and Economic Science at the London School of Economics. You can find out more about this material at: https://booth.lse.ac.uk/learn-more. The collection includes information about identified individuals. Booth's team was particularly interested in the most recent large-scale immigrant group, Eastern Europe Jews. Some of the material has been digitalised. For example, you can see the notes taken during an interview with Mr Zeitlin, secretary of the Jewish branch of the Amalgamated Tailors Society, 9 December 1887. Below are the notes made following an interview with the Secretary of the Hebrew Cabinet Makers' Association, 1888:

> The Society had only been in existence about 12 months. It had about 50 members of whom 40 were free of benefit. The subscription is 4d per week. The benefits were 18/- a week for sick pay and 10/- a week when out of work. A man when out of work would have to sign the register daily. If a man is out of work as a result of neglect or through any fault of his own, he would not be paid. The only expenses the Society had to

meet besides payments to members was an allowance of £3.00 per annum to the Secretary for expenses etc.

The Society was formed to the men many of whom were unable to speak the English language and consequently were imposed upon by the masters. Now, when there was a dispute between the masters and the men, the Secretary would undertake to look after the men's interests. Had two cases of this sort.

The society was not strong enough to influence the trade yet and was disliked by the masters. Men had been discharged for belonging to the Society.

The interview with the Hebrew Cabinet Makers' Association Secretary, 14 March 1888, can be found in the Charles Booth Collection, Booth Notebooks B81, fo. 41 in the British Library of Political and Economic Science.

The personal testimony of solidarity below comes from Robert Leeson's 1973 collection of personal testimony from union activists, *Strike*. Alf Garrard recalled hearing about trade-unionism in the trenches of the First World War. After the war he got a job in Lambeth and joined the Amalgamated Society of Woodworkers:

> Almost at once we were involved in a lockout in the shipping industry, paying a levy of six shillings a week. Then came the movement for 44 hours, '44 and no more'. We were working 52 hours in the building trade. Every morning we would send our pickets to building sites all over the area to see that 44 hours were worked and no more. On one job, the foreman said 'At half past five I shall blow my whistle', and we told him 'At half past five you can blow your bloody brains out and there'll be nobody to hear you'. Every day at 5 o'clock somebody would strike a girder and that would be a signal for every bit of metal on the job to be banged. So much so, in fact

that the local hospital sent a deputation to the shop stewards to ask them to lay off. In the end the firm gave in and the whistle went at five o'clock.

Sometimes people who were not members of a fraternal body can illuminate the motives of those who were. Rosina Bruce joined the Castle Laundry in Putney in 1923. Her recollections indicate some of the difficulties faced by women who wanted to join a trade union and reveal something about her relationship with her father and perhaps about working women's confidence. Even if your ancestor was not one of those recorded, you can gain an insight into working lives.

> One day the union men waited outside for us and gave us leaflets to join the union. When we went back in the laundry the manager, Mr Simpson, stopped the machinery and said 'If any of you join the union you can collect your employment cards on the way out'. We all went silently back to work. When I told my Dad he said 'You should have all walked out'. When I said we needed the money and were afraid of losing our jobs he tried to explain the power that workers had if they stuck together for better conditions. He really got frustrated at times at the ignorance of the working people who thought the bosses were doing them a favour by employing them.

During the Second World War Rosina was on piece-work, paid according to the amount of ironing that she did.

> There were nine of us and I was elected to ask for more money as we ironed and folded pyjamas for 4d per dozen. I asked for 6d per dozen. The supervisor said 'Who else is complaining?' Not one of the girls I worked with looked up. And so she said 'Alright, as it's only you, get your cards'.

Rosina got another job soon afterwards, as it was wartime and there was plenty of work. She only returned to laundry work in 1951. This material is in Jo Stanley and Bronwen Griffiths, *For Love & Shillings. Wandsworth Women's Working Lives* (1990). A useful tip for family historians is have a look at local history books for evidence such as this.

Chapter 3

PRESS REPORTS

Having considered personal accounts and collections you could next turn to the immediate area where your ancestor lived. In this chapter the focus is first on how local events were recorded. The second section is about how to be a critical reader, alert to the omissions and slant of the materials you assess.

LOCAL STORIES
Local newspapers are a useful source for reports on local events. They can also provide opinions about local, national and sometimes international issues. You can find out about meetings, court proceedings, speeches, election campaigns, local government and businesses in the area in which you are interested. Editorials and letters to the editor might give insights which you cannot find elsewhere. Fraternal bodies are often mentioned, with individuals named in obituaries and speeches quoted, sometimes at length. For example, the *Belfast News-letter* of 22 November 1860 reported a 'Masonic soiree' held in the Court House, Carrickfergus. The account includes a list of some of those present. The names and rank (there were three vicars, three captains, two doctors) of fifteen men are given and there are details of an address on 'The advantages of education' and a talk on 'the utility and principles of Freemasonry as an institution'. Newspapers also carry reports on funerals, sometimes detailing which organisations were represented and information about the deceased. An obituary of Ralph Dawes, 1920–2008, a member of the Royal Musgrove Lodge of the Oddfellows

quoted Mr Dawes and appeared in *Parish News, covering Shillington, Pegsdon and Higham Gobion*, No. 74, February 2008. After photographs became relatively easy to reproduce, newspapers began to provide images of local people and sometimes ran series on 'notables' giving biographical details.

You can find many newspapers online as well as in local record offices. After the British Library Newspaper collection in Colindale closed in 2013 the newspaper microfilm collection was moved to the British Library at St Pancras, London. It is located in the Newsroom on the second floor, https://www.bl.uk/visit/reading-rooms/news room. You can gain access to microfilm and digital newspapers and some archived websites. Print newspapers are in the National Newspaper Building at Boston Spa, West Yorkshire. If you make a request at the British Library in London and give 48 hours notice, copies will be produced there. There is a free help and advice service, https://www.bl.uk/help/free-discovery-and-1-2-1-sessions. In addition to the main copyright collection of British Library newspapers, http://www.bl.uk/reshelp/findhelprestype/news/index.html, there are collections in the National Library of Wales, the National Library of Scotland, the National Library of Ireland and the Belfast Central Library. You can also go via The National Archives at: http://www.nationalarchives.gov.uk/help-with-your-research/research-guides/newspapers/. There is also the British Newspaper Archive. Before making a payment, you can check the catalogue to see what your newspapers will be. You can search newspapers by date, country, region, county (do remember that some county boundaries have altered significantly over time), place and recently added titles. Some libraries and archives have institutional subscriptions which enable you to read for free once you are in the building. See: https://www.britishnewspaperarchive.co.uk/.

National newspapers' reports can provide a different perspective on the news. You may be able to access newspapers through your local studies library. Bear in mind general issues about access to archives in terms of open times. *The Times* is available online:

http://gale.cengage.co.uk/times.aspx/. Libraries that subscribe allow you to read back copies online for free. Copies of the *Observer* (first published 1791) and the *Guardian* (from 1821) can be viewed via a subscription service: https://theguardian.newspapers.com. Many libraries subscribe and allow you access via ProQuest: https://search.proquest.com. Apart from a few articles removed for copyright reasons (e.g. a book serialisation), content that has appeared in the *Observer* and *Guardian* in both print editions and online since September 1998 is available at: https://www.theguardian.com/uk. The English, Scottish and Irish editions from the past nine months, as well as a lot of other publications, are available at: https://www.backissuenewspapers.co.uk. There are also newspapers on the Historic Newspapers site. It advertises itself as 'the world's largest archive', https://www.historic-newspapers.co.uk. For press coverage of memorable moments see here: http://memorablemoments.co.uk. You may find the mode of access an issue. If there is no digital access, you might have to search through a vast number of printed copies, or more likely microfilm or microfiche. Some repositories do not have local newspapers available in a digital format. Coverage is uneven. For example, The National Library of Wales website is useful for newspapers prior to 1919 but the *South Wales Argus* has never been digitalised.

Printed material may use very small, densely produced print. If you are using a microfilm reader you may be able to enlarge the print to the size you want. There may be arrangements for you to photocopy the material either yourself or by staff in a local archive. If permitted, a phone camera to iPad camera can be practical. This means that you can enlarge the image later. It is often useful to take the photograph off-centre, as otherwise the bright central backlight in the film reader can reduce the contrast between the print and the background. Sometimes online you have options for the size of the material on screen and you can select columns. If you are searching online, you'll be able to use the search terms to help you search for key people, dates and times and key events. If you get an unmanageable number of returns, this might be because the search has picked up on characters and parts of words. You may need to narrow your range of terms or select new ones. Sometimes it is worth searching for key words used in reports using an online database. Before starting a search through newspapers try to narrow down the dates between which you intend to search. For example, local elections were often held in November so a search in October will often tell you if a trade-unionist was standing for the local council. Once you start looking at a newspaper you will soon see that sport always tends to be in the same place, as do advertisements and editorial comment. Some places had both weekly and daily, morning or evening, newspapers and sometimes newspapers changed their titles. Once you are familiar with the local pattern your reading of the press will speed up.

POETRY AS A SOURCE

Press reports often provide not simply an account of a specific event but also enable you to learn about the context and the atmosphere of the time. Below is part of a poem recited at an Oddfellows ball in 1842. It was reproduced in a local newspaper and might have been read as an advertisement for the Oddfellows. The poem reminds readers of the slogan of the Oddfellows – 'Friendship, Truth and Love':

> To you, ye brethren of a sacred band,
> Whose deeds bear witness for you o'er the land,
> Ye who go forth the widow's home to bless,
> Ye who are fathers to the fatherless,
> Ye who march onward in benign crusade,
> And the pale realms of woe and want invade,
> Waging with poverty untiring war,
> Benevolence your ever-guiding star,
> Whilst a proud banner floats your ranks above,
> Bearing your watchwords, 'Friendship Truth and Love'

Sometimes the same local event will be reported in more than one newspaper. The *Leeds Mercury* reported that on 7 August 1860, in front of 40,000 people, the stone was laid for North Riding Infirmary 'in due masonic form' by the Earl of Zetland, the Lord Lieutenant of the Riding, who was also the Grand Master Mason of England. The Bishop of Ripon spoke, there was a collection for the new hospital, a procession, which included the Freemasons, the Oddfellows, the Free Gardeners and a number of other friendly societies, and a banquet in the Odd Fellows Hall. The account in the *York Herald* described the Masonic rituals performed and notes that a phial containing coins and a vellum scroll were deposited and that the engraved plate which described the occasion noted that the stone was laid 'with full masonic form'. It also reported the 'gay and glittering costumes of the Freemasons', listed the names of many of the 150 'gentlemen' who attended the banquet and reported on the speeches given. There was also a newspaper report that the stone was soon moved and the money, about 7s., and the parchment were stolen. You might also note also that several local titles had more than one edition, depending on locality. The most convenient library or online source may not have the one you need. An account of the ceremony for the laying of the foundation stone of the North Riding Infirmary, mentioned above, appeared in the *Darlington and Stockton Times* but this is not available online through the British Library.

PRESS BIAS

Newspapers, then and now, are often biased. Many were businesses which felt threatened by trade unions. Some trade unions ran their own newspapers so that they could counter the bias of the commercial press. Some events will not be reported, some will be reported with such derision and inaccuracy that you will need to work hard to decide what is likely to have occurred. It can also be difficult to work out where the newspaper got its information and to understand the local context. Until 1906 the two-seat constituency of Stockport had been held by a Liberal and a Conservative. The

The Zulu and Afghan Wars
AND
The Liverpool Victoria
Legal Friendly Society.

THE ZULU WAR.

Mr. WILLIAM BRYANT, of 37, Upper George Street, who lost his son in the terrible massacre at Isandula, writes to Mr. JOHN JONES, London Manager of the LIVERPOOL VICTORIA LEGAL FRIENDLY SOCIETY, 1, Finsbury Square, as follows:—
"I think it a duty to your society to thankfully acknowledge the promptitude with which you have paid the claim arising from the death of my son, Sergeant S. BRYANT, of the 1st Battalion, 3rd Regiment of Natal Native Contingent, who was killed in action at Isandula Hill, on the 22nd of January last, and who had been a member of your society for a short time. The claim was paid at your office immediately on the production of the certificate of the Hon. EDWARD WINGFIELD, Assistant Under Secretary of State for the Colonies; and I gratefully make this known that others may be induced to join your society, and participate in its benefits."—*The Weekly Times, April 8th, 1879.*

LYMM, NEAR WARRINGTON,
May 5th, 1879.
To the Officers of the LIVERPOOL VICTORIA LEGAL FRIENDLY SOCIETY.

GENTLEMEN—I beg to thank you most sincerely for the promptitude with which your Agent here paid me the claim of insurance on the life of my son, WILLIAM ROSCOE NEWTON, who was killed at Isandula, Cape of Good Hope, on January 22nd; and further to thank you for procuring the official documents from the War Office necessary for the payment of the sum of Assurance, thus saving me from all trouble, which, under the circumstances, I gratefully acknowledge.
I remain, Gentlemen, your obedient servant,
(Signed)   HANNAH NEWTON.

LYMM, NEAR WARRINGTON,
April 19th, 1879.
MR. GIBB.
DEAR SIR,—I am very thankful to you for having instructed your Agent here to pay me the insurance on the life of my son, JOHN WORRALL, who died in the Koorum Valley, Afghanistan, on the 16th of last February. Mr. SKILLING paid me immediately on my application.
I remain, dear sir,
Your obedient servant,
(Signed)   SARAH WORRALL.

The advantages of assuring with the LIVERPOOL VICTORIA LEGAL FRIENDLY SOCIETY cannot be over estimated. Assurances can be effected upon any Age, from One Week to Seventy-five Years, and Policies are issued for any sum not exceeding £200.

Since its establishment, the Society has paid in **Claims** and **Grants** nearly **Half a Million Sterling**.

The **Annual Premium Income** is **One Hundred and Fifty Thousand Pounds**.

The **Accumulated Capital** is over **Two Hundred and Twenty Thousand Pounds**, which belongs exclusively to the Members.

The Society has Agencies in almost every town throughout the United Kingdom. For Rates of Assurance see other side.

By order of the Committee of Management,
ROBERT GIBB, Secretary.
Chief Office—23, Islington, Liverpool.

Offices for Sunderland, 37, Robinson Street—W. S. REED, District Manager.

Collectors Wanted.   Liberal Terms allowed.

The Anglo-Zulu War occurred in 1879 and the Second Anglo-Afghan War was fought 1878–80. This Liverpool Victoria Legal Friendly Society advertisement emphasised that payments made, following the death of soldiers who were members, were swift. Moreover, the Society had large funds and 'agencies in almost every town'. It also took the opportunity to advertise for staff, the final line noting 'Collectors wanted'. (Author's collection)

The teetotal Independent Order of Rechabites, Salford Unity, magazine focused on its central concern. This was not its friendly society functions but its abhorrence of alcohol. Many friendly societies were specialist, just as many Freemasons' lodges and unions were. (Author's collection)

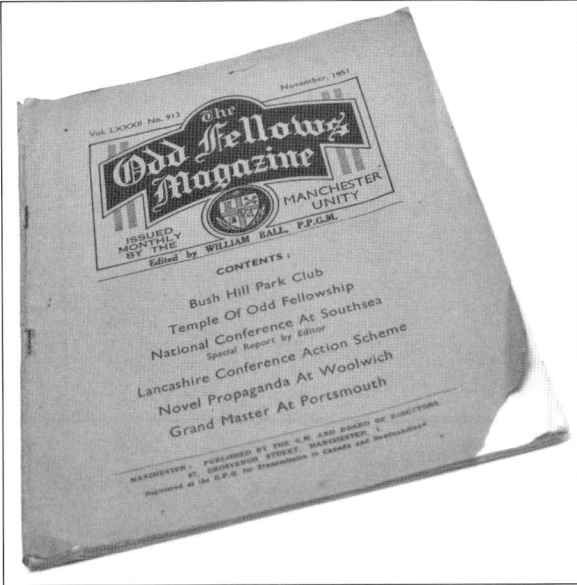

Magazines such as this one provide lots of local details, pictures and evidence of members' activities. (Author's collection)

Liberals and Labour then arranged a pact and won the seat. George Wardle had been a railway clerk for many years and then a newspaper editor, first for *Keighley Labour Journal*, 1893–7, and then, in a paid post, 1897–1917, for the *Railway Review*. This was the official paper of the rail union the Amalgamated Society of Railway Servants, which existed from 1872–1913. He was elected as a Labour MP, 1906–20. The *Cheshire Daily Echo* called the parties the 'Radicals and the Labour-Socialist party' and argued that their agreement denied the Conservative voters a representative in the Commons. It reported divisions, 'we hear signs of disapproval and dissention from the ranks of the Liberal Party and there are not a few members of the Labour Party who object this hobnobbing with the Radical'. The newspaper reported splits in the union between supporters of Wardle and those further to the left. Other fraternal bodies have also felt that they were presented in an unflattering light. In June 2018 Dr David Staples, the new CEO of the Freemasons' United Grand Lodge, England announced: 'My appointment signals a change in direction [. . .] One that is not content to be misrepresented by the popular press, or tolerate the slurs of the uninformed, but will stand up for itself'.

Newspaper accounts can be supplemented. At the Austin Motor Company (later part of British Leyland) union membership grew from about 10 per cent to well over half of the workforce during the Second World War, when it was difficult to sack union officials. After the war the union enjoyed uneven success, with a severe setback for the National Union of Vehicle Builders in 1953. In 1956, after the company announced a large number of redundancies, there was an effective strike. By its conclusion the Longbridge plant was almost entirely unionised. Dick Etheridge, 1909–85, a convener of shop stewards at the Longbridge motor works near Birmingham for over thirty years from 1941, kept records of his union activities. These can be found in the Modern Records Centre, University of Warwick. There is more about the MRC in Chapter 7. *The Dictionary of Labour Biography*, Vol. 9, has an entry on Dick Etheridge. *The Dictionary of Labour Biography* is a series of volumes with a large number of editors. The first volume was published in 1972 and Vol. 14 in 2018. Etheridge's version can be compared with the account of a strike at the Austin plant at Longbridge from a newspaper. The *Manchester Guardian*, 25 July 1956, described mass picketing by thousands of workers at the main gate on the previous day:

> The magistrates, M G Reeve and Mr J Bolus, who are the Chairman and Secretary respectively of the local district of the Confederation of Shipbuilding and Engineering Unions, said that they were going to protest to the Chief Constable about the action of the police. The central disputes committee also said that it had received a number of complaints that the police were provoking incidents and causing disturbances and that a deputation would protest to the Chief Constable. The Committee said that the police outside Tractors and Transmissions had been using their fists on pickets, that

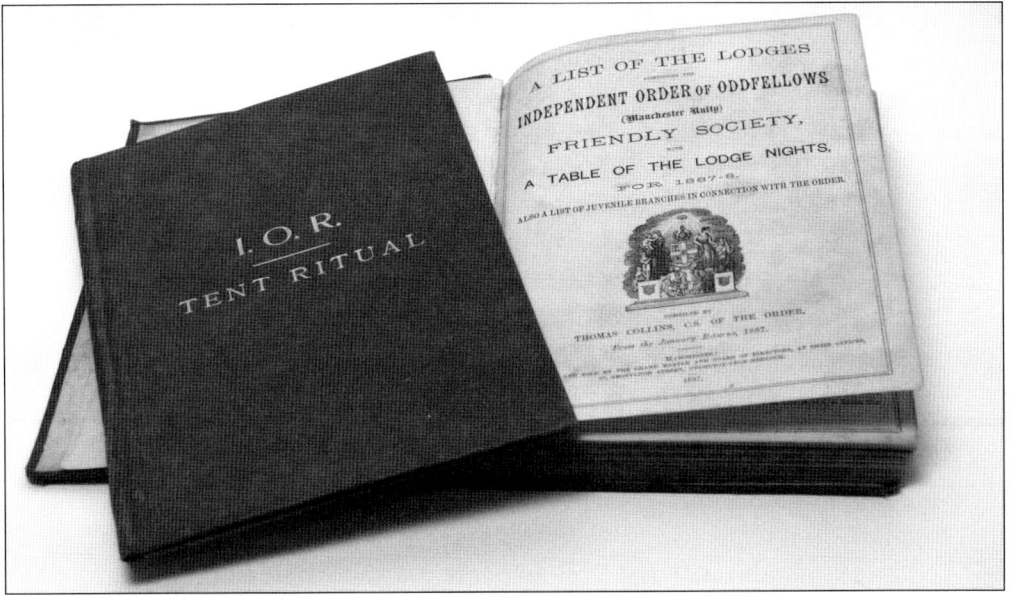

Available via online auctions, ritual books and lists of lodges can provide lots of information about the activities of your ancestor. (Author's collection)

mounted police had 'charged' a line of pickets at Fisher and Ludlow, and that at the Austin works the police had been actively assisting lorries to get into the factory and prevent the pickets from doing their proper work.

On 25 July there was a struggle between pickets and police. Dick Etheridge recalled:

The police came in, in force. I had the door of one truck open to speak to the driver, when one police officer got hold of me, one of the special police holds, and had me down on the ground. Suddenly like magic, he led me go. One of our lads, a former paratrooper, put a certain hold on him. The men and women lay down in the road and stopped the trucks. It was rough for a while, but by the second day we started to build up. The news came, the number was out, then that one. We got together and marched around the place singing what became our Austin's anthem, 'Keep Right On to the End of the Road', and the departments came out one by one. In the end we won and we marched back, as we'd come out, dropping the workers off at each department, singing to the tune of 'Marching through Georgia'. 'Hurrah, Hurrah, we've beat the BMC'. We were out for two weeks, followed by two weeks holiday. They agreed to make redundancy payments and to take people back as things picked up, which they did.

There are numerous official histories, memoirs and academic accounts of trade unions, friendly societies and Freemasonry. While these will all have their own biases, many contain fascinating details of lives and work practices. Even if you do not find a reference to an ancestor in the text or in a photograph, you may well be able to find out what their work or membership activities involved and gain clues as to why they joined the lodge (be it Masonic, union or friendly society) and remained within it for so many years.

Chapter 4

FRATERNITY BEFORE ABOUT 1800

In this chapter three phases of development are outlined. There are roots in the ancient world of the Greeks and Romans and then there is consideration of the medieval trade, craft and religious guilds and thirdly the social clubs and the specialist box clubs, sick clubs and benefit clubs that existed in the eighteenth century and which came to be called friendly societies in the 1780s.

THE ANCIENT WORLD

Friendly societies and the Freemasons often claim to have origins in ancient Egypt, or in the Kingdom of Solomon or among the Knights Templars. In 1909 a Provincial Grand Master of the Oddfellows claimed 'that Adam was an Oddfellow no one can doubt and that Eve was another is a matter of fact; and that they constituted in the Garden of Eden the first Oddfellows' Friendly Society is a matter of History'. In 1842 the same society's Board of Directors asserted that the name of Oddfellows was granted by Titus Caesar in 79 CE. Tales such as these were one way that fraternal bodies reminded members of their longevity, reliability and respectability. They also boldly declared to the world that as far as the fraternal body was concerned how it got to where it was today was not a matter which should be left to somebody else. This body could engage with building an understanding of the relationship between past and present. While you cannot expect to trace your ancestry back to ancient Greece and

Rome, an understanding of the roots of the fraternal bodies helps us to gain a sense of their attractions to your ancestor.

For centuries people recognised the benefits of mutual aid and of structuring that support so as to give a greater sense of security. In Roman times soldiers and artisans in specific trades formed mutual aid organisations. Members would make payments to their societies and the societies would make payments when members were ill and towards their funeral costs. Roman *collegia*, trade groupings, provided burials for members and existed across the Roman Empire. The Roman god Mithras was the central figure of a fraternal cult which was popular among Roman soldiers in Britain and elsewhere from the first to the fourth centuries of the Common Era. Mithraism was an initiatory order, passed from initiate to initiate, and there were seven degrees of membership, following the initiation ceremony. In 43 CE the Romans arrived in Britain and within a few years the city of London began to be built. By the third century a stone Temple of Mithras was being used there. Excavated by archaeologists in 1954, it was relocated to permit building work and in 2017 it was put on display in a new museum, the London Mithraeum, as part of an exhibition space beneath a new building. A partial reconstruction of this temple can be found 7m below the modern pavement level in Bloomberg's European headquarters, in Walbrook, in the City of London.

The Romans not only built mutual aid bodies for men, they also developed other ideas that have informed fraternal bodies, notably valuation techniques, the law of contract and the notion that it was the right of the state to intervene in economic matters. The existence of annuities can be traced back to Roman times when those who sold marine insurance arranged contracts for payments for a fixed term or for life. A table of annuity rates was calculated in about 230 CE. The Romans also had a goddess of justice, Iustitia, who had scales for weighing out justice and a sword for enforcing it. Sometimes she also has a torch, the light of truth, and a bundle of rods, the fasces, which cannot be broken when united. From

Roman sources fraternal bodies could have taken a number of their enduring images.

GUILDS

Many fraternities were suppressed following the adoption of Christianity in the fourth century CE. Others adapted and became the basis for guilds, a type of organisation that flourished in Britain under the Normans. Although there were discontinuities, the fraternal bodies considered in this book have roots in medieval guilds. Guild members visited sick members, paid alms from a common chest, attended funerals, imposed fines on those who failed to attend or whose behaviour was not respectable, and often elected their officials and held annual feasts. There is evidence of charitable feasts being held before the first millennium.

During the medieval period specialist societies, such as craft guilds, developed, but there were also religious fraternities, members of which might had have a variety of jobs. These associations were organised to provide for members who were unable to work due to fire, theft or old age. There was also a long-standing tradition of these guilds honouring their dead and of members dressing in regalia on parades and providing for widows and orphans. Although assisting the needy was seen as a means of improving an individual's prospects of reaching heaven, guilds were often discriminating. They favoured members over others and the deserving over the undeserving. Guilds provided charity for their members and held collective religious observances, feasts and processions. Some medieval parish guilds held annual banquets for paupers in honour of patron saints. Members had a duty not only to pay their subscriptions, but to attend events including funerals. In that they promoted collective self-help, Christian morality, elections, costumes, feasting, ceremonies and visits to the homes of the recipients of largesse, medieval and early modern religious and craft guilds can be seen as the parents of friendly societies and charities. Guilds took a variety of forms but among their most frequently expressed aims were fellowship, charity, commerce, conviviality, and a commitment to endow members with trading privileges. For most the central function was to enable men to assemble in order to ensure the welfare of both members and others. Although not the only source for the tradition of such charitable feasting as fundraising dinners and 'charity ales', the annual banquets of medieval parish guilds, which were held in honour of patron saints, involved sharing with paupers and celebrated, in the view of guests, a spirit of solidarity, friendship and peace. As such, they were a significant precedent for later fraternal bodies.

The Reformation of the 1540s saw the end of most religious guilds in England. Their property was confiscated and the Statute of Apprentices, 1563, removed their regulation of apprenticeships. The early twentieth-century historians of the labour movement, Sidney and Beatrice Webb, saw the industrialisation of the nineteenth century as a break from the past and trade unions as distinctive from guilds. However, subsequent studies have noted that craft guilds were maintained, their ideas spread and that they were of considerable relevance to the regulation of trade during the eighteenth century. Women's membership of guilds was often through marriage. Through guilds women were able to participate in the market economy. The similarity of guilds' rules among the weavers of London, Oxford, Marlborough and Beverley and the existence of merchant and craft guilds with reciprocal agreements to fraternal bodies in different towns indicates the existence of networks, some of them across conventional social and class lines. In this way fraternal bodies can be seen as the basis of communities.

Records of convivial mutual insurance schemes in Scotland date from at least the 1550s. In 2011 the General Register Office for Scotland and The National Archives of Scotland merged to form the National Records of Scotland. This body collects, preserves and produces information about Scotland's people and history. See https://www.nrscotland.gov.uk. It holds the records of the Brotherly

Society of Coopers of Leith, the Tranent Benevolent Society of Colliers and the Inverness Cabmen's Union. There are some list of members. See Ian MacDougall (compiler and ed.), *A Catalogue of some labour records in Scotland and some Scots records outside Scotland* for the Scottish Labour History Society (1978). Friendly society records for Free Church ministers can be found in NRS reference CH3/515-517. There are also some records relating to early trade-union activity. JC26/ 250 relates to the trial of James Granger, who, in 1788, was charged with entering into a combination to raise the wages of weavers. The Lord Advocate's Department holds the records of the Scottish Weavers Association, 1808–13. These were seized as part of the preparation for a trial. See NRS reference AD14/13/8.

DRAMA
Roman theatre developed traditions of dream and nightmare scenes and medieval guilds' morality plays were infused with allegorical and symbolic drama, as were Christian rituals. In both Greek theatre and the Catholic Mass, the audience, congregation, was offered the possibility of transformation as a result of participation in a sacred drama. These principles are shared by many fraternities which engage in ritual drama. In the case of the Freemasons, members re-enact morality plays based on the building of Solomon's Temple by the architect Hiram Abiff. Through role play, props and the use of all the senses, Freemasons associated with Grand United Lodge, England tell the story of how Hiram Abiff's secrets were lost when he was murdered for refusing to divulge the Masonic password. Members are reminded of the inevitability of death and importance of a lifetime of fidelity. Learning the scripts and playing the parts is said to develop a sense of mutual support. Members can be identified by their knowledge of signs and passwords unknown to those who have not sworn to keep them secret. This gives meetings a sense of mystery. Drama has long had the capacity to generate awe and surprise, to promote bonds between those who have been

initiated and to keep members alert over the course of their membership.

Friendly societies also had initiation rites. These opportunities for ritual and drama may have frightened as well as informed. Members of the Operative Society of Builders wore regalia and carried gilded axes. The initiation ceremony for the Operative Stonemasons' Society involved blindfolding. Between 1810 and 1825 the First-Degree initiation within the Oddfellows began with the blindfolding and binding of the candidate, the baring of his breast and his passage into the lodge between two Guardians who made challenges. He heard the rattling of chains and was sometimes thrown into brushwood or had his head immersed in water. When his blindfold was removed there was a sword pointed at his heart. The man holding the weapon asked the members assembled, who were robed and masked, if he should be merciful. Once they had decided to be merciful the candidate was sworn in, unbound and shown a figure of Death and other symbols. The Ancient Order of Foresters, formed in 1834, developed from an older body, the Royal Foresters. They symbolically fought with swords at an initiation. This was changed to clubs and then fighting was forbidden when the ritual was modified in 1843.

A number of medieval fraternities, with their feasting and processions based on those of the Catholic Church, disappeared with the Reformation of the 1540s. The property of religious guilds was confiscated. However, guilds continued to be of importance, holding feasts and processions, with regalia and rituals. They reached a post-Reformation peak membership in the period 1700–20 and then declined. There were also records of box clubs from the 1600s. Members paid into the box, often held in a pub, and payments were made from the box in the event of sickness or a funeral.

Freemasonry probably developed when declining medieval stonemasons' guilds recruited gentlemen with an interest in a range of legends, rituals and mystical practices. It can be dated to about 1425 when the Regius Manuscript was composed. This poem described the duties to which Masons had to swear on admission. It may have been a response to a ban on meetings by Masons. There have been Masonic lodges in Edinburgh since at least 1599, there are minutes from that year and there are claims of earlier Masonic activity. There are references to lodges and Freemasonry since at least 1646 in England. In 1717 four London-based lodges formed the first Grand Lodge. By 1740 there were over a hundred London lodges (branches) of the Freemasons, several score in the provinces and nine abroad. A group of Irish Masons formed a rival Grand Lodge known as the 'Antients' in 1751. The inaugural Grand Lodge became known as the 'Moderns' or 'premier'. The Grand Lodge of Scotland was created in 1736 and had about 326 warranted lodges. There were between 700 and 800 lodges in Ireland. The number of members in each lodge had also grown over the century. Freemasonry flourished and was popular with men from a wide range of backgrounds and professions. Accounts of the origins of Freemasonry have been much disputed. If your ancestor was a Mason he would almost certainly have heard and discussed these matters.

In 1600 by the age of 15 most people lived away from home, often working as servants while saving for their own marriages and household. There was less reliance on family networks and a greater expectation that men would support their wives while older people would, if it was required, receive care through Poor Law provision. The legislation for the relief of the poor passed in 1598, 1601 and subsequently made clear the responsibilities of parishes and encouraged labour mobility. Knowing that there was provision for the subsistence of all subjects, even in the face of local crises, provided a basis that encouraged people to consider the broad issues of welfare, health and responsibility for the strangers in their midst. This bolstered the development of bodies to run pooled insurance schemes such as the friendly societies. In medieval Scotland St Crispin and his brother St Crispianus became popular with cordwainers. There is a record of a St Crispin Society in 1763. A Royal St Crispin Society emerged in about 1817 and an associated network

Freemasons have long worn elaborate aprons to lodge meetings. An illustration of 1723 shows one being worn. There have been many materials and a huge variety of styles since that time. Some Freemasons are initiated into more than one lodge and some join Masonic bodies known as 'additional degrees' or 'side degrees'. These are some early side degree aprons. From Aubrey Newman, David Hughes and Don Peacock, Freemasonry in Leicestershire and Rutland. The 'Other' Orders and degrees, The Provincial Grand Lodge of Leicestershire and Rutland, Leicester *(2012).*

There is a distinctive apron for each of the three ceremonies that introduce a man to Craft Freemasonry, each more elaborate than the last one. The side Order aprons are often even more ornate. This side Order apron features the first and last letters of the Greek alphabet, alpha and omega, which are often used as Christian symbols. (Reproduced from Aubrey Newman, David Hughes and Don Peacock, Freemasonry in Leicestershire and Rutland. The 'Other' Orders and degrees, The Provincial Grand Lodge of Leicestershire and Rutland, Leicester *(2012))*

This side Order apron one has the words 'Salix' and 'Nonis' written clockwise around the central image. Both words are said to be formed from the initial letters of a Masonic secret. They are also associated with a Masonic system popular in France and the USA, the Ancient and Accepted Rite. This admits only Trinitarian Christians.

Freemasons wear aprons when they attend ceremonial meetings of the lodge. After becoming a Freemason some members join additional, often specialist, Orders. These Orders often have their own regalia and focus. This is an early Masonic 'side Order' degree apron. These aprons can vary widely in style, shape and material, for example, lambswool or silk. This one has a crucifix-type cross and skull and crossbones (often called a memento mori, or reminder of death). Dating such items is not straightforward as the symbols have been in use for centuries.

of lodges was created in Scotland. Members of this Scottish working men's association practised rituals based on shoemaking legends and traditions until the Society closed in 1909. While the Society owed something to Freemasonry, it also had elements associated with trade-unionism and friendly societies. If your ancestor was a member of a fraternal body in Scotland then, through the Scottish Archive Network's online catalogue (electronic database), you can search over 20,000 collections in 52 Scottish repositories, http://www.scan.org.uk.

THE LONG EIGHTEENTH CENTURY
A further incentive to join a fraternal body was that, as industrialisation and urbanisation increased and the population grew, men sought new identities and developed new rituals of civility, fellowship and trust. After the Glorious Revolution of 1688, socially mobile and relatively prosperous male newcomers to the new towns sought security by making bonds with other men. They recast the idea of collecting money and making payments to the sick and to widows and of having feasts and social meetings. Modern fraternities have also been influenced by the Huguenots, persecuted Protestants who escaped from France in the seventeenth century, bringing their associational cultural forms with them. Greater access to print and changes in communication enabled the notion of fraternity to be reconstructed.

Men started to form clubs, and the sprinkling of such establishments in 1688 grew swiftly after that date. One commentator noted in 1720s that London had 'an infinity of clubs or societies', while in 1732 another writer felt that no village or town was without such clubs. These were for those interested in self-improvement, music and a whole range of activities. The value of such associations was so ubiquitous that in 1725 heaven was visualised as one large friendly society. Clubs, meeting in coffee houses and pubs, became the secular successors to, and substitutes for, church. If your ancestor joined, then it might have been because a club provided access to a fantasy and exclusive world. Oxford was home to numerous dining and social clubs such as the Eternal Club and also the Jelly Bag Society. Members of Oxford's Town Smarts wore white stockings, silver buckles and frilly shirts. Other clubs catered to those interested in poetry, bell-ringing and a range of other activities, while there were also the Anti-Gallicans and the Irish and Welsh clubs. In Edinburgh women could join, among other bodies, the Fair Intellectual Club, founded soon after the Act of Union, while in Maidstone there was the Maidstone Society for Useful Knowledge (members included Benjamin Franklin, the Sanskrit scholar Sir William Jones and the agriculturalist Arthur Young). There were also societies for those interested in agriculture, music, cards, cricket, books and politics as well as benefit clubs and a Masonic lodge. By the mid-1790s there was both a radical Corresponding Society and an opposing Loyalist association. Up to 20,000 attended the 2,000 or so clubs every night in London (or so it was claimed). Many of these clubs folded and those which survived often developed elaborate rules and protocols which helped members to gain a sense of fellowship.

After initial hostility from the Church and government, by the mid-seventeenth century Royal Charters were being granted to these organisations. The Society of Artists was chartered in 1765 and the Royal Academy three years later. In Scotland, the beneficiaries included the Royal Society of Antiquaries (1783), the Royal Society of Edinburgh (1783) and the Highland Society (1787). Through admission strategies and self-promotion these clubs built on fashionable fellowship to mobilise opinion, spread information, promote collaboration between men otherwise unlikely to meet. They offered social cohesion, a spreading of power and support for the nurturing of a variety of skills. For further details about the growth in clubs in England from about 150 to over 6,500 between 1700 and 1790, see Chapter 9 of Peter Clark's *British clubs and societies 1580–1800: the Origins of an Associational World* (2000).

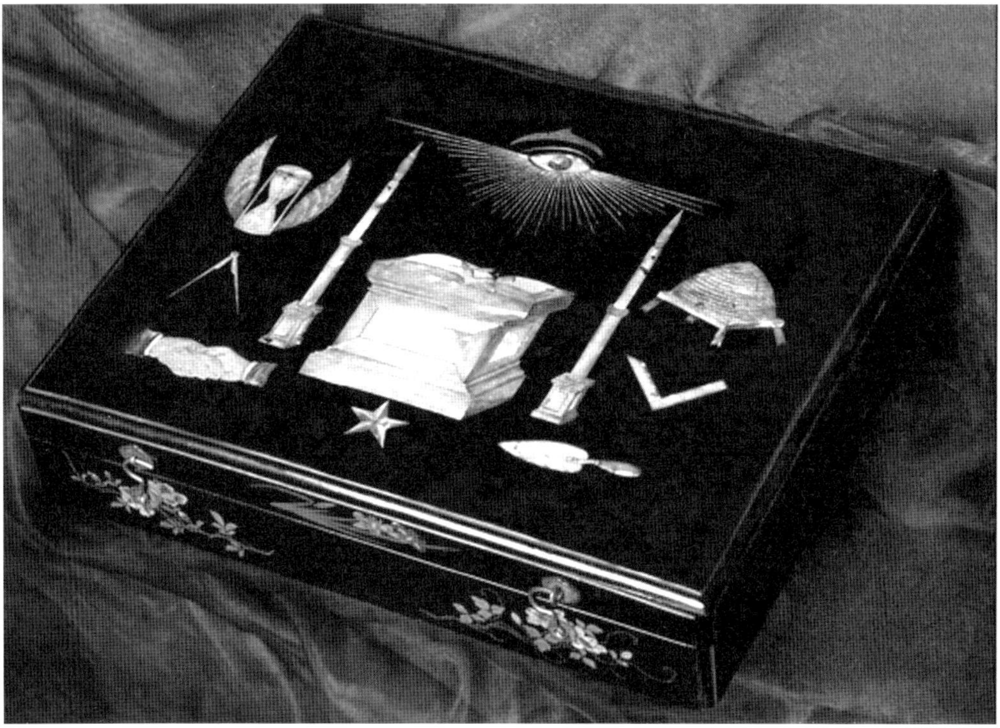

Your Freemason ancestor might have joined more than one lodge of Freemasons and more than one Order. He may well have acquired several aprons and other items of regalia. He would have got changed into these items in the lodge. This case for carrying regalia is decorated with frequently illustrated images associated with Freemasonry, notably the square and compass. It is the case belonging to a member of the Knights of Malta Lodge which has been meeting in Hinckley, south-west Leicestershire since 1803.

Early Masonic aprons were individually made and styled. However, industrialisation saw a recourse to mass production and conformity. This is a copper plate used to print aprons.

Fraternity Before About 1800

In 1753 the Unanimous Club was founded by a wealthy Freemason, Thomas Golightly, in Liverpool and in 1797 an Athenaeum Club was established in the same city. Members included Freemasons George Canning, who was briefly prime minister, William Ewart, MP 1828–68, and Viscount Leverhulme, the soap baron who built Port Sunlight. Gentlemen's clubs, in addition to offering a place to relax and exchange ideas and possibly influence local decision-makers and climb the social ladder, often promoted similar ideas to those of Freemasonry regarding architecture and philanthropy. Such clubs became very popular in the eighteenth and nineteenth centuries. They tended to have little by way of ritual, though there were traditions of toasting during meals and after-dinner speeches. There were around 1,000 clubs in London by 1760 and, across the English-speaking world, perhaps 25,000 by 1800, including around 7,000 friendly societies with an estimated 660,000 members. In 1804 there was a benefit club to every 710 people in the north-west of England and each club had an average of 87 members. Many of these friendly societies combined the activities of insurance, savings and trade-union activity.

While fraternal bodies have been formed for a variety of purposes, religion, mutual aid and conviviality remained prominent. A notion of fraternity could link people across social and economic divisions and tie individual, familial and communal survival strategies and security to social activities and secrecy. Often structured using terms associated with families, such as fathers and brothers, the origins of many present-day fraternal bodies lie in these organisations. If your eighteenth-century ancestor was a relatively well-off and literate man living in a town, there is an excellent chance that he was a member of a club. If he was less wealthy, he may well have been a member of a box club.

Chapter 5

FREEMASONRY

This chapter sets out the development of Freemasonry since about 1800. Freemasonry has long been a powerful presence in Britain and abroad. Outsiders often regard the international fraternity, with its elaborate secret rituals, as an alien and inherently hostile institution, although this image might have been attractive. Freemasonry's influence on the Enlightenment and Western culture, especially in the eighteenth and early nineteenth centuries, was vast. Masonic ideas permeated the design of buildings, parks, gardens and cemeteries. While this chapter is chronological, there are some diversions to consider Freemasonry and Christianity, specialist lodges, regalia, women in Freemasonry and Freemasonry's social and international roles. There is also discussion as to how to engage with both Freemasons' own understanding of their past and how others have presented Freemasonry.

Freemasonry has helped to bridge social boundaries and to foster Enlightenment ideas about order and society. It has attracted royalty, industrialists and prime ministers to its ranks and in the nineteenth century the number of lodges around the British Empire, and beyond, grew. The offer of ritual, self-improvement, charity, insurance and social services to members and others appealed to many. While today we might see the restrictions and gaps in the idea that Freemason brothers could only meet 'upon the level', if they were freeborn men aged over 21 who had no physical disabilities, in the past Freemasonry was a challenge to conventions. Even today it is not always accepted. Through the act of becoming a Freemason your ancestor may have been making a number of statements about himself and his identity. However, it was Freemasonry's efforts to avoid suppression which are perhaps of most interest to researchers. This is because in order to avoid being banned as a seditious organisation the Freemasons agreed that members' personal details would be recorded. Today many of those records are available online.

> **BECOMING A CRITICAL READER**
> The UK's largest secular, fraternal and charitable organisation, Freemasonry, has been subject to much speculation. Although defined by its central organisation in England as 'a system of morality veiled in allegory and illustrated by symbols', there is a lot of material in print and online that suggests that it is a powerful, evil, force. In his book *The Devil's Dictionary* (1911), Ambrose Bierce satirised the conspiracy theories:
>
>> FREEMASONS, n. An order with secret rites, grotesque ceremonies and fantastic costumes, which, originating in the reign of Charles II, among working artisans of London, has been joined successively by the dead of past centuries in unbroken retrogression until now it embraces all the generations of man on the hither side of Adam and is drumming up distinguished recruits among the pre-Creational inhabitants of Chaos and Formless Void. The order was founded at different times by Charlemagne, Julius Caesar, Cyrus, Solomon, Zoroaster, Confucious, Thothmes, and Buddha. Its emblems and symbols have been found in the Catacombs of Paris and Rome, on the stones of the Parthenon and the Chinese Great Wall, among the temples of Karnak and Palmyra and in the Egyptian Pyramids – always by a Freemason.
>
> Since 1911 the number of unproven claims about Freemasonry has risen. Freemasonry has, like many other groups, faced

> difficulties with inclusion and membership as well as organisational and social challenges. Unlike other social or recreational bodies, such as the local tennis club, it has been thrust into public awareness by the novel and film *The Da Vinci Code* (2006). There are numerous websites offering fantastical speculations and conspiracy theories. Some of these sites connect the Freemasons to the Templars, Gnostic sects, satanic brotherhoods, spiritualists, Pythagorean Orders, Rosicrucisans and the Priory of Sion. Despite the dire warnings on many sites, these ideas need only be taken as seriously as the 1995 episode of the US-based animated television series *The Simpsons*. This introduced the Stonecutters, an organisation with a male-only lodge, rituals and a song that foregrounded the allegations of powers of societies with secrets.

Having grown in status in the 1700s, by the end of the century, when there were about 500 Modern lodges, and about 270 Antient ones, Freemasonry was subject to allegations of complicity with revolution. The Irish rebels of 1797 were said to have organised in Masonic-type organisations. Anxieties about the role of secret societies cast a long shadow over Freemasonry. Perhaps to demonstrate innocence and loyalty, the Lodge of Lights in Warrington became a branch of the local militia. In Sheffield, Masonic lodges split after a dispute about the use of the Masonic hall by the radical Sheffield Society for Constitutional Information. The Home Office received reports on proceedings in Masonic lodges in Leeds. Members of a lodge in Brentford were accused of plotting to kill the king.

To try and keep control, in 1793 the government gave some associations, friendly societies, legal standing under the Act for the Relief and Encouragement of Friendly Societies. This was followed by the Treason Act 1795. This required that organisers request a magistrate's licence for events involving public discussions or a lecture. The Seditious Meetings Act 1795 was intended to limit the size of public meetings to fifty people. Further restrictions were passed. The 1799 'act for the more effectual suppression of societies established for seditious and treasonable purposes, and for better preventing treasonable and seditious practices' was aimed at radical bodies such as the London Corresponding Society and the United Irishmen. These had arisen in response to the French Revolution of 1789 and favoured large-scale social and political change. Although there was some evidence that Freemasonry was used as a cover by Irish republicans, the Freemasons sought exemption from laws that banned them meeting together. This was granted but, from 1799 until 1967, lodges of Freemasons were obliged by law to register their membership with the local Clerk of the Peace. The Combination Acts of 1799 and 1800 were aimed at trade unions and collective bargaining. They also indicate governmental wariness of men gathering together. Some Masons were arrested under these laws. Cotton spinner John Haigh was a member of the Lodge of Friendship in Oldham, 1818–49. He was gaoled for radical activity in 1812 and 1820. He was later a Chartist, campaigning for the right to vote, 1838–41. James Macartney was a member of the Masonic Royal Grove Lodge, Soho and a compositor on *The Times*. When he was imprisoned for nine months in 1810, under the Combination Acts, United Grand Lodge, England, supported his wife and children.

In 1813 there was a union of the two rival Masonic grand lodges in England. They formed a new governing body for Channel Islands, Wales and England freemasonry: United Grand Lodge of England, UGLE. Constitutional changes were made with officers given more precisely defined duties and powers. Below UGLE were Provincial Grand Lodges and individual lodges. There was a similar structure in Scotland, Ireland and elsewhere. Men aged over 21 (or over 18 in the case of two Oxford and Cambridge lodges) could join and advance by degrees, that is by showing proficiency and understanding in Freemasonry. They could serve as officers, such as secretary or warden and become a Worshipful Master and then on to other lodges of Mark Masonry and Royal Ark Mariners. One aim was to

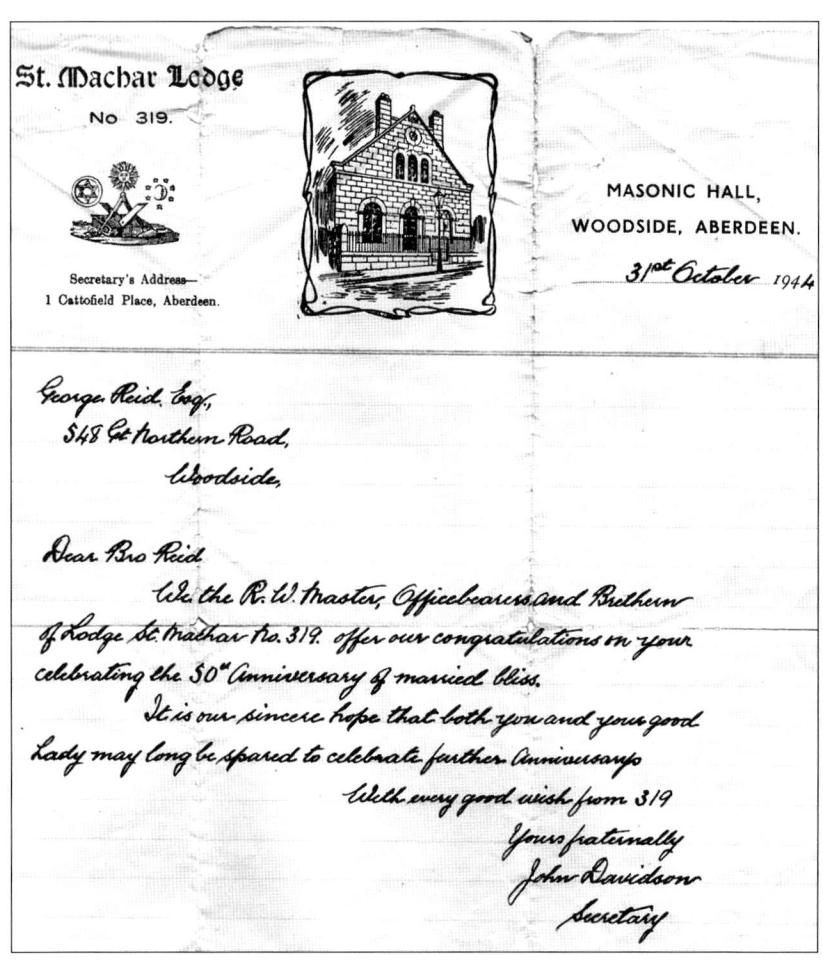

This letter was written in 1944 by the Lodge Secretary of St Machar Lodge, No. 319, in Aberdeen. On behalf of the senior officer, who, in lodges under the Scottish Constitution, was known as the Right Worshipful (here RW) Master and the Officebearers and brethren, the writer offered congratulations to George Reid on 'the 50th anniversary of married bliss'. George's wife, called 'your good Lady' in the letter, was May, who came from Kemnay, which is about 14 miles from where the couple were living in 1944. They had both travelled separately from Scotland to the USA where they met. In 1894 they married in Vinal Haven, Maine. Founded in 1826, from 1904 the lodge met in the purpose-built meeting place illustrated on the letterhead. It was about half a mile away from George and May Reid's home. George, a highly skilled stone dresser and sett maker, and his son helped to maintain the lodge while May's two brothers ran a building firm in Kemnay and erected the local Masonic hall which is still home to St Bryde Lodge, No. 991. (© Graeme Reid of Aberdeen)

demonstrate that Freemasonry was not seditious and could be the basis for a new uniform order which could spread across the Empire. Some were still not welcome in the newly unified United Grand Lodge, including freed slaves (which caused difficulties in the Caribbean) and some of those associated with the industrial north. Several lodges in the north-west of England seceded following the Union.

If your ancestor was in a fraternity you might well find evidence in the graveyard. This is a Masonic headstone in St Mary De Castro churchyard, Castle View, Leicester. (© Andy Green)

RECORDS
Following the 1799 legislation, records of Masonic membership were retained with other information within the Quarter Sessions records series. Many are accessible at local record offices in England and

Grave in Kemnay, Aberdeenshire. Alexander Clarihew of Kintore Aberdeenshire trained in the local granite industry in and around the city of Aberdeen in Scotland. Entering the trade at 15, he was an accomplished stone cutter and dresser by the time he was 20. He emigrated to the USA where he helped run the granite business Clarihew & Gray until ill-health overcame him and he returned to Scotland, where he died. Buried in the graveyard at Kemnay, famous for its granite, his gravestone is a fine example of the granite cutter's art. The Masonic emblems indicate his engagement with that fraternity. (© Graeme Reid of Aberdeen)

Wales. You are advised to use the online catalogues of libraries and archives before you visit and to book a visit. The websites often provide information about parking, accessibility and where you can get a coffee when you need a break from looking at old documents. It can be useful to ring in advance to check on the availability of the material you wish to see and to check if you will be permitted to photocopy or photograph it. Some records are incomplete and many are fuller for the earlier nineteenth century than later. Each record reveals name, profession, residence, date of initiation or date the person joined, age at initiation and lodge location. When military lodges' regiments were stationed in Britain they placed their certificates with local Quarter Sessions. A list of annual returns known to exist in local record office collections was made and details are available at: http://freemasonry.london.museum/it/wp-content/ uploads/2011/02/Records-relating-to-freemasonry-in-Quarter-Sessions-Records.pdf. The law was not strictly enforced during the latter part of the period. In 1920 the London Clerk of the

Peace estimated that only half the lodges made returns and Grand Lodge felt obliged to remind lodge secretaries to make their returns. In 1939 Counsel's opinion confirmed the view of a Clerk of the Peace in Essex who pointed out that lodges founded before 12 July 1799 were exempt from the Act. The Attorney General agreed not to prosecute Freemasons' lodges under the Act but lodges continued to provide data. Eventually, in 1967 the legislation of 1799 was repealed.

In some record offices you may well find additional data, about Royal Arch membership, or lodge minute books, Treasurer's accounts, attendance books, membership rolls, letters and photographs of members in regalia. A list for a Lancashire lodge in the Quarter Sessions records includes information about members' height, complexion, hair colour, eye colour and tattoos. This anomaly was perhaps the work of a Secretary who wanted to record that Freemasons were fit enough to fight during the Napoleonic Wars. The 1799 Returns in Worcestershire have details often omitted from returns to Grand Lodge such as full addresses and addresses of businesses linked to members. As they were done annually they are also useful in identifying social change in members and occupation changes. For example, a member was a keeper at his initiation becoming a hop merchant and ended up as a 'gentleman'. There are also examples of additional data entries made in a more recent period. For example, a list of eighteenth-century freemasons in Sunderland has been compiled from library and museum membership registers. See: http://www.durhampast.net/ sunderland_masons.htm.

Lodge membership data is also held centrally. Freemasons' Hall is located at 60 Great Queen Street, London WC2B 5AZ. The library and museum there holds the archives of UGLE. It has examples of numerous artefacts, all the major Masonic periodicals of the nineteenth century, papers relating to Masonic buildings and charities and some chapter and lodge records. For a fee you can request that research be done on your behalf. It can be contacted on

020 7831 9811, http://freemasonry.london.museum/library-museum-archive/. There is an online catalogue which includes details of most printed and some archive resources, see: http://www.freemasonry.london.museum/catalogue.php. This should be consulted prior to a visit to the library and museum. All researchers must register.

Details transcribed from lists of lodge members in the Quarter Sessions records at Essex Record Office are also available. Included are details for members between 1799 and 1900 and searchable lists of lodges, surnames and professions in the county, http://www.southchurch.mesh4us.org.uk/oaths.php. When data from two sample lodges was compared with pre-1813 annual returns and membership registers at the library and museum, it became apparent that they included additional names, not found in Grand Lodge membership registers. There is a 10 to 15 per cent discrepancy between names sent to the clerk of the peace and now at Essex Record Office and those sent to Grand Lodge of Essex lodge members listed in the Quarter Sessions returns during the late eighteenth and early nineteenth centuries. This occurred predominantly in seafaring towns such as Harwich and army towns such as Colchester, where new members were initiated quickly before departure overseas, and depended on the accuracy of secretaries when sending records and when they were obliged to do so. Sometimes lodges initiated, passed and raised a candidate on the same day (a process usually taking several months) to ensure a membership certificate could be provided. Names may not have been included as this was a way to avoid making capitation fees, i.e. payments towards Masonic charities and Grand Lodge administration.

For over 2 million Freemasons within UGLE and the Grand Lodge of Ireland the dates of joining or initiation, the ages and the lodges of which they were members in England, Wales and some overseas areas (those which were part of the Empire) have been digitalised for the period 1751–1923. You can access this data via www.ancestry.co.uk, an online family history resource which is available by subscription or via some libraries and archives. These include UGLE's library and museum. These records include data about jobs and you can see the social class of Freemasons. There were 14,882 'Gentlemen', and numerous merchants, engineers, clerks and farmers. Antients Grand Lodge membership started in 1751. Most entries include details of name and membership fees paid. Moderns' membership registers began in 1768 and include names, dates of joining or initiation and subsequent membership history but only occasionally profession. Lists of members' names were included in the lists of lodges in the Moderns Grand Lodge minutes for 1723, 1725 and 1730. Details for surviving annual returns before the Union of Antients and Moderns in 1813, from which these early membership registers were compiled, are included in the library and museum online catalogue and are fully accessible. Access to the fragile original membership registers is not permitted but, in most cases, digital copies of the registers until 1887 are available. Membership records, arranged not by surnames but according to lodge name and number, were standardised after the Union in 1813. They include information such as date of initiation or joining, full name, age, address, details of other lodges or chapters joined, fees paid and, of prime importance for family researchers, occupation or profession.

For England you can search by lodge in other ways. The UGLE is in charge of the first three or 'Craft' degrees of English Freemasonry. A closely connected, but separate Order is that of Royal Arch. It is a continuation of Craft Freemasonry with members ('Companions') meeting in a chapter under a Grand Chapter. The Supreme Grand Chapter of England is the governing body of Royal Arch Masons in England, Wales and the Channel Islands and is based in the same building as the UGLE. It is not clear when it started but Royal Arch was known in London, York and Dublin by the late 1730s. Royal Arch data cannot be found through Ancestry but the Research Service at UGLE can help with chapter details.

On occasion the annual returns provide missing details about members that were not transcribed into the membership registers. Data about members that can be compiled from these sources is not comprehensive. Some additional membership information, membership lists, minute books, declaration books, has been gleaned from printed lodge histories and lodge records and is available in the library and museum. Copies of the *Masonic Mirror*, *Freemasons' Quarterly Review* (later *Freemasons' Quarterly Review and General Assurance Advocate*), the *Freemason*, *Freemasons Journal* and *Freemasonry Today* can be consulted at the UGLE library. The *Review* reported discussions in the Grand Lodge. As there were disputes as to the accuracy of the accounts, helpfully for historians, minutes of debates in Grand Lodge began to be kept. By the mid-century provincial yearbooks were being published and Provincial Grand Masters had gained greater status. Sometimes both soldiers and prisoners of war would attend local lodge meetings and UGLE also has records of all the UGLE Freemasons who died in the forces during the two world wars.

Finding out when and where lodges met is facilitated by searching the electronic version of John Lane's *Masonic Records 1717–1894*. Originally published in 1895, it has now been updated and is available on an online searchable database of all the lodges established by the English Grand Lodges from the foundation of the first Grand Lodge in 1717 until 2010, http://freemasonry. london. museum/resources-information/lanes-masonic-records/. It is also available at: http://www.freemasonry.dept.shef.ac.uk /lane/. Records are covered by a restricted access period of seventy years and a charge is made to retrieve this data. Details of more recent lodges can also be found via the Library and Museum of Freemasonry.

REPUBLICAN FREEMASONRY

Your ancestor might have preferred the different approach to Freemasonry adopted by the French. Charles Bradlaugh (1833–90) was an atheist who, in 1859, joined Grand Lodge des Philadelphes, an irregular French Masonic lodge meeting in London, and three years later joined a regular lodge in Paris. Records in the Library and Museum of Freemasonry and in Bradlaugh's own papers (at the Bishopsgate Institute, http://www.bishopsgate.org.uk/content.aspx?CategoryID=1519) show that he joined a lodge near his north London home. In 1874, when the Prince of Wales was nominated for the post of Grand Master, Bradlaugh, a republican, resigned from English Freemasonry. When elected as an MP in 1880, he was prevented from taking up his seat for six years as he was not permitted to take the oath of allegiance. However, he maintained his connections with French Freemasonry. Although there are no central records of Freemasons in France, there have been several studies of Freemasons in specific regions. In 1966 Alain Le Bihan produced an inventory of the Parisian Freemasons of the Grand Orient of France, in 1988 Joël Coutura produced a biographical dictionary of Masons in eighteenth-century Bordeaux. In 1998 Éric Saunier published data about 6,000 Freemasons in Normandy between 1740 and 1830, while Jean Crouzet published a study of Basque Masons. More recently there have been studies of Masons in Rennes, 1748–1998 and also of Lyon in the eighteenth century. Jean Bossu collected data on 165,896 Freemasons of the period 1750–1850. The data is available both in the French National Library and online in the Bossu File: http://fichier-bossu.fr/. There were also lodges for French prisoners held during the Napoleonic Wars. Some Masonic collections contain jewels or tie-pins made by French prisoners of war during the period of the Revolutionary and Napoleonic wars. Despite the fact that the two countries were at war with one another, these were often purchased to assist brethren in distress.

> They sometimes come up at auctions. For more on this topic see Mark Dennis and Nicholas Saunders' *Craft and Conflict: Masonic trench art and military memorabilia* (2003).

Philip Crossle's *Irish Masonic Records*, published by Grand Lodge of Ireland, Dublin in 1973, lists lodges that were active under the Irish Constitution between 1760 and 1973. This cannot be viewed online but Grand Lodge of Ireland membership registers are available via Ancestry. The Grand Lodge of Ireland is the governing body for the whole of Ireland. It has archives and a museum with records and photographs in Freemasons' Hall, 17–19 Molesworth Street, Dublin 2, https://freemason.ie. Researchers seeking access to complimentary information about lodges in Scotland can refer to George Draffen's *Scottish Masonic Records, 1736–1950. A list of all the lodges at home and abroad chartered by the Grand Lodge of Scotland, Lodge Mother Kilwinning, Lodge Melrose St. John with the dates of their charters, places of meeting, alter actions in numbers and colour of clothing, 1950*. This lists lodges of the Scottish Constitution between 1736 and 1950. See: http://freemasonry.dept.shef.ac.uk/?q=resources_draffen. The Grand Lodge of Scotland records are not available online. However, the Grand Lodge of Scotland, Freemasons Hall, 96 George Street, Edinburgh EH2 3DH, has a genealogy department with guidelines and information about Masonic war memorials in Scotland, http://www.grand-lodge.net/asp/mwmform.asp. Other Masonic war memorials can be found through online searching. Grand Lodge of Scotland administers Scottish Freemasonry including provincial and district grand lodges and local lodges.

CHRISTIANITY
Although Freemasons have no sacraments, dogma or offer of salvation there is some common ground with Christianity. In 1813 the Antients, which emphasised a link with Christianity, accepted the Moderns' practice of omitting specific references to Christ or the Christian faith. The Duke of Sussex, a younger son of King

George III, became Grand Master and a period of standardisation and consolidation followed. Joseph Smith Jr of the Church of Jesus Christ of Latter-Day Saints was made a Freemason in 1842 and Masonic teachings appear in Mormon doctrine. Marriages have been reaffirmed in lodges and there are rituals relating to deceased Masons. The lectures designed to support the learning and reflection required to become a master Mason, or for additional degrees, can be understood as different levels of consciousness within the psyche or in religious terms. Members are encouraged to embrace moral standards relating to brotherly love, relief and truth and to participate in costumed, ritualistic myth-telling ceremonies incorporating symbolism and role play. Some Christian traditions have been of influence but there are Freemasons from a number of faiths. Often lodge meetings involved songs sung to hymn tunes. Masonic traditions came to reflect the popularity of religious sentiment across Britain.

Since 1738, when the Pope wanted to excommunicate Freemasons, the Roman Catholic Church has been overt in its criticism of Freemasonry, Continental Freemasonry having been identified with liberalism and anticlericalism. By contrast, although some Protestants have expressed alarm about Freemasonry, many have embraced it. English Freemasonry has long been associated with conservatism, establishment and religion. In the early 1950s, both King George VI (the Head of the Church of England) and Geoffrey Fisher (Archbishop of Canterbury) were Freemasons. Nevertheless, in 1951 doubts about the compatibility of Freemasonry and Christianity were raised in both the Church and the press. The popular newspaper *Reynolds News* ran with the headline: 'Church of England Sensation: King May Act in Row over Freemasonry', and there was a motion in Parliament calling for a Royal Commission to inquire into the impact of Freemasonry on the political, religious, social and administrative life of the country. On publication in 1952 Anglican clergyman Walton Hannah's book, *Darkness Visible:*

A Christian Appraisal of Freemasonry, received a lot of publicity. One *Daily Mirror* headline read: 'Secret Signs of a Million Men'. If you are investigating your ancestor who was a Freemason in this period you might bear in mind that sensationalist reporting could have determined how secretive that ancestor was about being in a lodge. The anonymous 'Vindex' responded to Hannah with *Light Invisible: The Freemasonry Answer to Darkness Visible* but in this there is no denial (or confirmation) of the precision of the description of rituals. The Church decided that Anglicanism and Freemasonry were compatible and by 1953 it was clear that, in addition to the Archbishop of Canterbury, sixteen Anglican bishops were Freemasons. Moreover, King George VI praised the beneficial influence of Freemasons, stating: 'The world today does require spiritual and moral regeneration. I have no doubt, after many years as a member of our Order, that Freemasonry can play an important part in that vital need'. He had joined Navy Lodge No. 2612 in 1919, accepted the charge of the Masonic province of Middlesex in 1924 and was installed as Grand Master Mason of the Grand Lodge of Scotland in 1936. He was also Head of the Church of England. The Archbishop retired in 1961 and in 1964, more than a decade after the Bishop of Woolwich had appealed for reform, lodges were permitted to change the oaths so as to make clear that none of the references to grotesque ways of killing, which were part of the drama, would be inflicted. However, many lodges retained the older oaths.

In 1985 a private member's motion in the Church of England's General Synod led to the formation of a working group. This followed the example of a Church of Scotland investigation. Members included two Freemasons and the working group received substantial evidence from the Grand Lodge and 106 written submissions. Its 1987 report, *Freemasonry and Christianity: Are They Compatible?*, came to a similar conclusion as its counterpart in Scotland. While there were concerns, no action needed to be taken to restrict Anglican membership. Correspondence in Church newspapers indicated both opposition and support for the outcome. People noted that the Freemasons were philanthropic, promoted beneficial networks and were often committed to their local church. There were also complaints that Freemasons were self-serving. Others felt that the matter was of little relevance, perhaps because by this time the Freemasons were seen as less influential. The monarch was not a Freemason and the Duke of Edinburgh has never been active. None of the princes have joined. The Duke of Kent, a cousin to the Queen, joined in 1963 and in 1967 became the 10th Grand Master of UGLE.

CHARITY

The 1830s saw a shift in direction for the Freemasons which may have been related to the English and Welsh legislation, 1834 Poor Law (Amendment) Act. This legislation led to a fall in government expenditure on poor relief by 50 per cent to 1 per cent of the national income. Individual parishes ceased to have responsibility for the poor. Instead, they were in the hands of local Boards of Guardians which had jurisdiction over areas known as Poor Law Unions. The poor could, under certain circumstances, be offered places in sex-segregated workhouses rather than be assisted while living at home. Inmates received free food and accommodation but life in the workhouse was often bleak so as to deter any but the truly destitute from applying to live there. The Freemasons reacted to the new Poor Law by running schemes to help keep members from the workhouse. They raised funds for an Asylum for Aged and Decrepit Freemasons through a new magazine, the *Freemasons' Quarterly Review*. As with friendly societies, charity was linked to self-help and security. You may find among an ancestor's records certificates issued to subscribers to Masonic charities. These include the Royal Masonic Institute for Girls, founded 1788, the Royal Masonic Institute for Boys, founded 1794, a charity for the children of Freemasons, the Masonic Trust for Boys and Girls. The records of the Royal Masonic Institute for Boys are not digitalised but the UGLE has minutes, reports, correspondence, photographs and other records. There was also a range of other charities including the Royal Masonic Benevolent Institution, which was established in 1850, and the Royal Masonic Hospital, which opened in 1933.

Freemasonry continued to expect members to support charities for both Masons and others. Currently the Masonic Charitable Foundation helps gifted young people. Details of members claiming Masonic assistance are found in the records of the Lodge of Benevolence and associated charity petitions. There is guidance in Pat Lewis' *My ancestor was a Freemason*. This was published by the Society of Genealogists, and the 4th edition appeared in 2012. Note that this focuses on Freemasonry in England and Wales not Scotland or Ireland.

ORNAMENTATION
During the Victorian period the number of Masonic lodges within the British Empire quadrupled to almost 2,000. Freemasonry enabled members to cross social barriers. In England, but not Scotland and Ireland, the middle class took control of Freemasonry, building Masonic halls in city centres. Professional classes could socialise in their own space and lodges were developed for the police, for teachers and for members of the London School Board. The rise in popularity of Masonic ladies' nights from the end of the nineteenth century encouraged social interaction among families of Freemasons and their guests. Masons displayed expensive jewels and regalia, both in the lodges and when taking part in civic processions. The Masonic Knights Templar and Knights of Malta wore a medieval-style tabard (it was an apron in the nineteenth century), a cloak, cap and sword. Rank is shown by neck jewels and the style of badge worn on the cape. Although brethren might argue that fraternity was focused upon moral and spiritual values, material culture was employed to reinforce values within the lodge and outside. Elaborate regalia was displayed at ladies' nights and Masonic balls but there were also household objects with symbols on them. Snuffboxes, jugs,

warming pans and even jelly moulds might be decorated with fraternal symbols or reminders of central ideas. There were elaborate drinking vessels (tea cups for the temperance societies, beer mugs for others), jugs and punch bowls and all the utensils which supported smoking. You may find Masonic medals ('jewels'), aprons, collars, gauntlets and sashes and numerous ceramic items, such as jugs, all decorated with symbols. Sales of costumes, lodge furniture, rings, snuffboxes, walking sticks and other objects have soared. If you come across such items they can give you clues about your ancestor. You will often see acronyms such as WM (Worshipful Master). The WM is the senior officer in a lodge in England. In Scotland the title is Right Worshipful Master. This person is elected to chair lodge business and presides over rituals. At the conclusion of the limited term of office, normally a year, a Worshipful Master is termed a Past Master. The UGLE Museum and Library has material that indicates the meanings of many of these abbreviations and there are books offering guidance on the acronyms. There are jewels that are made available to WMs and Past Masters. If you find one of these, it indicates the status your ancestor acquired. Jewels also signify other honours or events.

SOCIAL BASE

The shift in the class base of Freemasonry in England can be seen from an examination of specific lodges. In 1800 there were about 524 lodges in England and Wales and 13,000 members. They were often small traders and skilled artisans, such as carpenters, tailors, bakers, shoemakers, stonemasons and printers. The Lodge of Friendship in Oldham also included working men, notably weavers, joiners, turners, blacksmiths and cordwainers. This lodge also made payments, for example, to support the ill wife of a member in 1792 and to imprisoned brothers and to victims of a burst reservoir and a boiler explosion. A coffin was purchased for a brother in 1816, a Benevolent Society in 1828 and a Sick Fund in 1829. There is evidence of members including labouring tradesmen in Crewe and in Macclesfield and of a travelling brother, who was moving from lodge to lodge, seeking employment or support. In the 1790s the Royal Yorkshire Lodge in Keighley, Yorkshire was dominated by labouring tradesmen. Then butchers, grocers and professionals began to join. By the 1840s local gentlemen, schoolmasters and manufacturers were in the ascendant. Studies of the social status of Provincial Grand Masters and of lodges in Wolverhampton and Leicester indicate that Freemasons and their officers were increasingly drawn from professional and business backgrounds. In the early nineteenth century members of the Freemason's Lodge of Lights, in Warrington, Lancashire (see Chapter 1), included weavers, a fustian-cutter, soldiers, excise officers and schoolmasters. In 1802 and 1812 there were collections to support Masonic brothers imprisoned for debt. In 1831 the lodge paid 8*s*. 10*d*. in relief payments to brethren but such payments became less frequent by the late 1840s. A local file manufacturer joined in 1846 and was soon followed by a surgeon, a solicitor and the Deputy Constable. Prominent local industrialists Joseph Stubs and Peter Rylands became involved and in 1850 Sir Gilbert Greenall (1806–94) joined. He was a JP, the MP for Warrington and heir to a local brewery. He went on to chair the family firm, 1880–94, and a Masonic lodge which opened in the town in 1869 was named Gilbert Greenall Lodge. His brother was the MP for Wigan and owned fourteen pubs in St Helens. He instigated the foundation of the first terminating building society in the town and became an Oddfellows Provincial Grand Master.

A similar picture of the social realignment of the Freemasons can be seen in the Philanthropic Lodge No. 107 which was founded in 1810 in King's Lynn, Norfolk. It was not the first Masonic lodge in the town, there had been at least six others, but it was the only one in existence in the town between 1851 and 1906. Membership levels over the period changed but in 1896 there were sixty-six members, making it the second largest of any lodge in the county. Initially the lodge was dominated by artisans and mariners. The cooper, the

Freemasonry

butcher, the carpenters, pilots, whitesmith, blacksmith and bakers all joined before 1840. The boatbuilders and shipwrights had left by 1815, the whitesmiths and pilots by 1818, the blacksmith by 1820, the cooper in 1829, the butcher in 1831, the carpenters by 1833 and the bakers by 1837. The wealthier seafarers, the captain, master mariners and naval officers, were all members between 1832 and 1842 and two master mariners remained after the latter date. Apart from one clerk who was a member between 1813 and 1816, clerks only joined the Philanthropic Lodge after 1839. There were four by 1873 and six in 1876. The first bank manager to join became a member in 1873 and, leaving aside one who was a founder member in 1810, the first brewer joined after 1887. A merchant joined in 1835 but he was the sole merchant until 1857 when two more joined. In 1875 a fourth joined, there were seven by 1878 and nine by 1881. There were four farmers in the Philanthropic Lodge by 1812 and there remained that number until 1873 when the number rose to five and soon afterwards to six. No cleric joined the Philanthropic until 1861. Soon others did and there were eight Anglican clerical brethren by 1876. Lodge members included both Conservative newspaper proprietor John Dyker Thew, who was Lynn mayor in 1871, 1876 and 1885, and draper Alfred Jermyn, a Methodist and Liberal mayor in 1897 who was knighted in 1919. The first 'gentleman' joined the Philanthropic in 1858. However, there were three or fewer gentlemen Philanthropic Lodge members until the 1870s. In 1878 there were eight gentlemen in the Philanthropic Lodge and nine by 1880. Moreover, a number of these gentlemen joined from other Masonic lodges. When the Prince of Wales became Grand Master in 1874 it signalled that Freemasonry was a means by which the Victorian middle classes could affirm its respectability and prestige. The Freemasons have produced lengthy lists of members famous for their drama, literature, music, political activities and contributions to science. Your ancestor may have wanted to rub shoulders with Oscar Wilde, Winston Churchill or Scott of the Antarctic.

Indicative of social changes within the Philanthropic Lodge is the shift in the occupation of the Worshipful Masters over the course of the century. John Whaley, a gunsmith, was one of the eight initiates of the Philanthropic Lodge in 1810 and the Worshipful Master in 1811, 1812 and 1814, while Sir William H. Ffolkes, the Worshipful Master in 1880, 1899 and 1910, owned the nearby, vast, Hillington estate. Another measure of the background of Philanthropic Lodge members is that in 1873 over 40 of them owned land in the county; 17 owned less than 20 acres each, a further 13 owned between 20 and 80 acres and 10 had between 100 and 500 acres. Robert Elwes owned 3,313 acres and while Granville Pitt did not own the 6,768 acres at Langley Park where he lived, his father did.

The possibility of social advance may have been an attraction of Freemasonry. In 1813, a Brazilian, Hippolito Jose da Costa, became the Provincial Grand Master for Rutland. The founder of a lodge in Ashby de la Zouch was blind from birth and the 'father of Freemasonry in Leicestershire', William Kelly, was the son of a hosier, who rose, despite his relative lack of wealth or rank, to become a Provincial Grand Master in the 1870s. A successor as Provincial Grand Master in 1913 was Edward Holmes, the son of a farm labourer. He was also the President of the Police Mutual Assurance Society and at his installation as Provincial Grand Master in 1913 the Pro Grand Master, Lord Ampthill, commented, 'there is nothing snobbish about Freemasonry'. Holmes was followed into office by a solicitor, whose grandfather had been a village labourer. If your ancestor was a Freemason, he might have felt proud of the prestige gained through his status in his lodge and he may have met men of higher social standing than himself through the lodge.

The interest in networking might have worked in more than one direction. Rural Norfolk had little by way of trade-union activity in the nineteenth century. The lodge may have offered opportunities for landowners to meet with workers in an informal manner. Moreover, even if a Freemason lodge was not a place to meet workers, the idea of encouraging fraternal societies may have appealed to Freemasons. Many Freemasons within the Philanthropic had links to other fraternal groups. Hamon L'Estrange, the Freemasons' Provincial Grand Treasurer, 1876–86, Grand Deacon and Grand Master, initiated an Oddfellows lodge in the town where he lived, Hunstanton, 17 miles from Lynn. John Rust, the Philanthropic Worshipful Master in 1892, was another Oddfellows Grand Master and Philanthropic member. James Lister Stead was also active in the Oddfellows. In 1866 Charles Theophilus Ives became Provincial Grand Master of the Lynn district of the Oddfellows and in 1867, seven years after he joined, he became Worshipful Master of the Philanthropic. Charles Edward Ward, a solicitor's clerk in Lynn, was a Master and Provincial Grand Senior Warden in the Freemasons, a patron of the Manchester Unity Oddfellows and, in 1906, the Ancient Order of Foresters Friendly Society (AoF) High Chief Ranger. Ward was married to an honorary member of a female Foresters Court (that is branch) which he had helped to found. Other Philanthropic Lodge members with links to the AoF included Richard Bryant, a Master and Provincial Grand Senior Warder and AoF National Committee member, Hamon L'Estrange, Sir W.H.B. Ffolkes Bart and Colonel William Pattrick (AoF Vice-Presidents) and two other members who were on the AoF executive. In addition, John William Hyner, a Master of the Philanthropic Lodge and Provincial Grand Registrar in the Freemasons, followed Ward and became a High Court Ranger. William Bennett, a Chief Ranger in the AoF Prince of Wales Court, worked for Philanthropic Lodge member John Dyker Thew. Using the records available via the UGLE Library you can build up a picture of the lodge of which your ancestor was a member and create a network of his associates. Perhaps he married the daughter of another Mason or went into business with somebody he met through the lodge?

In the lodges associated with Cornwall's copper and tin mining industries members with trade or manual backgrounds mixed with technical staff, professions associated with the middle classes or the local nobility. Almost 2,000 Masons were members of nearly 30 active lodges across Cornwall. Working miners as well as mine management were well-represented in the mining centres of Camborne and Redruth. In Chacewater there were 120 miners and 60 mine managers and engineers between 1857 and 1900. The lodge might have been where concerns which might have led to industrial conflict could be addressed and possibly resolved. While there were stoppages, no permanent union was popular in Cornwall's mines until the twentieth century. In the nineteenth century industrial unrest in Cornwall's copper and tin mines was uncommon. In 1866 the *Mining Journal* noted that a strike among the metalliferous miners of Cornwall and Devon was 'entirely unaccustomed'. By contrast, in South Wales and Yorkshire, trade unions attracted working men and the lodges were dominated by the middle class. In south Yorkshire's coal-dominated lodges mine managers and engineers made up about 20 per cent of the membership in the late 1870s but there were no ordinary miners. In 1880 in Barnsley the Friendly Lodge of Freemasons had no miners and three lodges in Wakefield were also middle class and included colliery agents, surveyors and managers but not miners. This was an area that was prominent in the development of trade-unionism for miners in the 1890s, and had more strikes than any other region in England. Cornish miners acted as strike breakers in some of the northern coal fields.

HISTORIANS OF FREEMASONRY
One of the earliest overviews of Freemasonry was provided by Robert Freke Gould. He was made a Freemason in 1855, aged 19. He became an army officer and later a barrister and maintained a constant interest in the history of Freemasonry. In the 1880s he was one of the Freemasons who established a new lodge for Masons interested in the history of their organisation, Quatuor Coronati Lodge. Members of this conduct research into the history of Freemasonry and there is a long-running associated journal, *Ars Quatuor Coronatorum* (AQC), https://www.quatuorcoronati.com.

Gould also produced his monumental three-volume *History of Freemasonry* (1883–7); this is available online at: https://archive.org/details/historyfreemaso00goulgoog and copies can be found via many second-hand booksellers. His follow-up, *Concise history of Freemasonry* (1904), is available online at: https://archive.org/details/ cu31924030281459. A searchable CD version was also produced, which can be purchased from the Archive CD Books Project at: http://www.archivecdbooks.ie/cgi-bin/sh000002.pl?REFPAGE=http%3a%2f%2fwww%2earchivecdbooks%2eie%2facatalog%2fall%2dbritain%2ehtml&WD=freke&SHOP=%20&PN=misc%2dlifestyle%2ehtml%23a1070#a1070.

For an overview of the development of Freemasonry John Hamill's *The Craft. A history of English Freemasonry* (1986) offers a view that benefits from an insider's perspective. David Harrison and Fred Lomax's *Freemasonry & fraternal societies* (2015) is also written with inside knowledge. They designed it as a 'quick guide' to non-Masonic Orders and an 'examination of the similarities between them and Freemasonry'. It is more than that as there is material on gentlemen's clubs, with particular reference to the north of England and also on the Druids, Buffaloes, the Ancient Shepherds, Free Gardeners and, to a lesser extent, the Elks, the Loyal Order of the Moose, the Society of the Horseman's Word and occult societies. In his *Freemasonry: a very short introduction* (2017), the former Director of the Centre for Research into Freemasonry and Fraternalism at the University of Sheffield, Andreas Önnerfors, outlines the history of Freemasonry and assesses its organisation, secrecy and rituals and the involvement of women.

There are also many lodge histories, often written by lodge members. Examples include Aubrey Newman, Donald Peacock and David Hughes' *A History of the Masonic Province of Leicestershire and Rutland* (2010) and W.J. Weedon's *History of the Lodge of St John No. 1370, 1870–1953* (1953). Many lodges have their own websites and some, such as that of the Provincial Grand

> Lodge of Cornwall, include brief histories of the lodge, http://pglcornwall. org.uk/home/history. These can provide additional information about the individuals. The Chelsea Lodge, formed in 1905, has included many entertainers within its membership and there is information about the activities of the lodge at: http://www. chelsea-lodge.org.uk. Another example can be found at: https: //www.stdavidslodge.co.uk. Before contacting any lodge it is advisable to find out as much as possible about the lodge from its website.

SPECIALIST LODGES

If you cannot find any evidence that your ancestor joined a local lodge, look further afield. While some lodges were based in specific towns or regions, others had members from all over the country, or indeed the world. Lodges dominated by men whose work took them to a variety of locations, such as railway workers or sailors, tended to be members of lodges where people from many places could meet and network. The first master of Scientific Lodge, No. 840, consecrated in 1860 at Stony Stratford, Buckinghamshire, was the superintendent of the London and North Western Railway's Wolverton works, which were nearby. Many of the members worked on the railways and came from a wide number of locations.

Some lodges implicitly restricted membership to men involved in particular occupations. Etruscan Lodge, No. 546, was consecrated in 1847 and based at Etruria, later moving to Longton at Stoke-on-Trent. Although lodge bye-laws did not restrict membership to those involved directly in pottery manufacturing, it established an association with the trade and an Etruscan vase image decorated its banner. The Liverpool Cotton Brokers' Association, founded 1841, had an associated lodge of Freemasons and the Association's President in the 1940s went on to become the Freemasons' Provincial Grand Master for West Lancashire in the 1950s. Covent Garden floristry traders were central to Hortus Lodge, No. 2469, formed in 1893, members of the London School Board formed a lodge in 1896.

Sir John Blundell Maple who owned the furniture maker Maple & Co. encouraged his staff and directors to join the Clarence Lodge of Instruction. William Hesketh Lever, 1st Lord Leverhulme founded several lodges in the vicinity of Port Sunlight, which was built by his company to accommodate workers in its soap factory. The Albert Edward Lodge, consecrated in 1875, was at one time known as a 'Doctors' Lodge. A lodge in a mining area, consecrated in 1892, attracted solicitors, surveyors, bank managers, factory owners and only two 'gentlemen', while in 1905 another was formed by those involved in public and civic affairs, including the mayor.

Members of the Authors' Lodge, No. 3456, which was founded in London in 1910, included Sir Arthur Conan Doyle, Rudyard Kipling, Henry Rider Haggard and Jerome K. Jerome. Masonic themes are threaded through several of Kipling's works and those of Rider Haggard, while Conan Doyle's *The Red-Headed League* (1891) is one of several Sherlock Holmes tales in which the hero indicates his familiarity with Freemasonry. The members of this lodge had met through the Authors' Club, formed in 1891. Another lodge, opened in 1926, was associated with the retail trade and there is also one that was initially closely associated with teachers. More recent specialisms include a lodge with many members in legal and financial institutions, as well as the local golf club, another for those in the footwear industry, one for former pupils of the same school and one for travelling showmen. Men in the tea trade formed Camellia Thea Lodge, No. 7351, in 1954, while those in the electric lighting trade formed the Lodge of Illumination, No. 7746, in 1960. There are the Gloucestershire Lodge of Agriculture, No. 9631, and Devonshire Emergency Services Lodge, No. 9613, the Sub Aqua Lodge, No. 9684, based at Uppermill, Yorkshire and Shokotan Karate Lodge, No. 9752, based in London. Harry Mendoza's *Serendipity: Musings on the Precedence of, and Numbers and Names Used by Lodges and Chapters of the United Grand Lodge of England* (1994) provides lists of lodges associated with particular professions and also lodge mottoes, names and banners.

Freemasons can rise through the rank to obtain a variety of grades within a 'degree'. Once a Mason has risen through the most popular of the degrees, the Craft degree, he might join additional degrees. There is a form of Freemasonry called Royal Arch Masonry. Members ('Companions') meet as a Chapter and Royal Arch confers four degrees. Royal Arch is the continuation of Craft Freemasonry.

In Scotland, where the owner of this watch lived, to qualify for admission to the Royal Arch one had to be a Mark Master Mason. In the USA, where the owner of this watch resided in the early nineteenth century, Royal Arch is part of the York Rite system of Masonic degrees. On the item attached to the watch are the letters H T W S S T K S. You might also see these letters on the gravestone of a Freemason. They are a reminder of how, as part of a ritual, a candidate carries a keystone with these letters on it to Right Worshipful Master. The latter explains that these letters stand for HIRAM, TYRIAN, WIDOW'S SON, SENDETH TO KING SOLOMON. This relates to a central narrative of Freemasonry and is part of a complicated and lengthy ritual. The story tells of how a Widow's son, Hiram, King of Tyre, in Lebanon was the chief architect of the temple for the King of Israel, Solomon. When he refused to reveal the secrets of Masonry he was murdered. On the reverse of the item pictured there is a triangle in a circle, which is part of the Royal Arch symbol. There are also some Hebrew letters which might have acted as a reminder of the tradition that Royal Arch Masons could gain access to the name of God, a name that is not supposed to be spoken. The original owner of this timepiece was George Reid of Aberdeen and this is evidence that he was a Royal Arch Mason who had risen to at least the Third Degree. The keystone is still in the Reid family and will be passed on to his great-grandson in the near future. (© Graeme Reid of Aberdeen)

Some specialist lodges subsequently broadened or become unviable. In Leicestershire one lodge sought to confine membership to gentlemen of the professions and only attracted nine men, another attracted the local militia and lapsed when, following the conclusion of the Seven Years War, the regiment was stood down. In 1929, because there was hostility between the Labour Party and the Freemasons, the New Welcome Lodge, No. 5139, was consecrated. Its purpose was to make Freemasonry more accessible to the working classes. Membership was largely made up of Labour MPs and officials. The intention was to improve relations between the new Labour government and Freemasonry. Within a few years the lodge's character changed, and membership eventually became open to all men associated with the Palace of Westminster.

As was noted in the case of the Philanthropic Lodge in King's Lynn, there are many other examples of Freemasons being active in other organisations. If you learn that your ancestor was a Freemason, do not stop there, but keep looking for other societies. The Hermetic Order of the Golden Dawn was an occult society formed in 1887 by Freemasons. This in turn led other members to become Freemasons. New York-born Arthur Edward Waite joined Isis-Urania Temple of the Outer Order of the Hermetic Order of the Golden Dawn in January 1891. Perhaps because of his familiarity with Catholic rituals, he seems to have been at ease there. He began to edit the *Unknown World*, 'a magazine devoted to the Occult Sciences, Magic Mystical Philosophy', wrote two novels and several books covering such subjects as ceremonial magic, Kabbalism and alchemy and the Holy Grail, and entered the Second Order of the Golden Dawn in 1899. Other members of the Order included W.B. Yeats, the Nobel Prize-winning Irish poet who served as an Irish Senator, and Arthur Machen, a popular Welsh author and mystic in the 1890s. By 1896 there were five Temples, over 300 members, women and men were permitted to join and a Second Order was created. In 1898 Aleister Crowley, the occultist, poet, novelist and mountaineer, joined the Order. It soon split into factions and Waite became a Freemason in

1901. He went on to write *A New Encyclopedia of Freemasonry* in 1921. This is only a brief glimpse of the complicated networks of occultists to demonstrate that your ancestor might have access to numerous varied connections through membership of fraternal societies.

Another possible attraction was that Freemasonry was thought to provide a link to ancient and hidden secrets. During the eighteenth and nineteenth centuries there was considerable interest in discovering the lost knowledge of the Egyptians. The creation, in 1811, of the London-based Egyptian Lodge of Freemasons reflects this curiosity. In 1852 Freemason Kenneth MacKenzie edited and translated Egyptologist Richard Lepsius' *Discoveries in Egypt, Ethiopia and the Peninsula of Sinai* and MacKenzie then wrote the six-part *Royal Masonic Cyclopaedia* (1875–7). In 1877 Amelia Edwards' popular *A thousand miles up the Nile* was published and in 1882 the Egypt Exploration Fund was established. The interest in revealing secrets from the past may have aided the growth of Freemasonry.

ASSESSING SOURCES

Given the reputation of Freemasonry, how do you find, collect and assess the useful material from among all the nonsense? One place to start is the collectively edited encyclopaedia Wikipedia. Although editors who are able control page structure and in certain cases 'lock' pages to prevent editing, in general anyone can add material to it. Nevertheless, Wikipedia is likely to get you a better answer than entering a query on a search engine (such as Google) and then considering the top hits that it finds for you. Wikipedia is often a good first step in a search, but hardly ever a good last step. It is most useful for dates, names, sequences, links and lists. It is less useful for current events, long-term events and definitions. It is better as a supplementary source rather than a main one. Wikipedia's editors request that contributors reference entries, but they only permit references to secondary sources, which includes some poorly written books. You can check the sources via the 'view source' tab. While many Wikipedia authors understand their own topic they may not be as good at understanding the broader subject. Some make exaggerated claims for their subject's significance within the wider context. This is sometimes the case with biographical entries. If you see the message 'This section does not cite any references or sources. Please help improve this section by adding citations to reliable sources. Unsourced material may be challenged and removed', then beware. Within the text sometimes editors draw attention to questionable assumptions by lacing comments in superscripted caveats. For example you might see 'He is said[by whom?] to have had a stable and comfortable childhood' or 'Passing his Entrance Exam with Distinction,[citation needed]'. Some entries have the sub-headings 'Controversy' and/or 'Criticism', which can give you access to a dissenting viewpoint on the main thrust of the article. If you click on the 'talk' tab you will be able to see a forum where the page's contributors can discuss it. This will help you see how the entry fits into the larger scale projects that Wikipedia is running. There is a rating system. You can see more via the Wikipedia page. The 'talk' page sometimes carries conflicting accusations. It can be difficult to work out which is the best source to trust, but you can get a sense of what not to trust. You might, for example, find that you can discover the birth and death dates of an individual, but that you remain uncertain as to that person's attitude towards socialism. The 'view history' tab reveals the previous edits to the entry. If you see that the word 'not' has been inserted recently into a sentence upon which you'd like to build, be careful. The 'Notes' at the end of the article show the footnotes for the entry and link to the References. There are also sometimes 'Lists' of other relevant Wikipedia articles. You can use these links to create reading lists but of course the quality of links can vary. Wikipedia allows you to assess the reliability of Wikipedia articles, to see what has occurred behind the scenes, but this is time consuming.

IMPERIAL CONNECTIONS

Freemasonry grew across the Empire. Those travelling out from Britain saw the lodge as a place where they could enjoy convivial company and possibly material assistance and social advancement. Freemasons fees tended to be higher than those of friendly societies. The initiation fee amounted to the equivalent of about two months' wages for a working man, and was equal to over a month's pay for a craftsman. Remaining a member cost about the same as membership of an Affiliated Order, that is a national friendly society. Members were expected to pay into the benevolence fund, to pay for entertainment and many went on to join additional lodges as a means to advance within the organisation. These side Orders of Royal Arch, Mark and Rose Croix offered more ritual. John Pearce Smith, a cooper in Cornubian Lodge, No. 450, of Hayle became Master in 1860, Provincial Grand Deacon in 1865 within the Freemasons, while innkeeper George Timmins became first Master of his lodge in 1880 and then Provincial Grand Assistant Director of Ceremonies by 1895. The Freemasons tried to maintain a degree of exclusivity. In 1900 the Grand Secretary reported that a reduction in initiations 'showed that the lodges were beginning to appreciate the fact that Freemasonry should be regarded as a luxury and not as a benefit society', and indeed relatively few Masons received benevolence, though there were schools available should their offspring be orphaned.

Despite the costs, membership of lodges in Cornwall increased in the 1870s when miners and mining engineers joined and then used their membership certificates as introductions to mine agents in South Africa, Australia, North and South America. Over 100 miners joined 3 mining lodges in the 1870s and a further 100 in the 1890s. Many then left for the goldfields of South Africa, taking their proof of membership with them in order to secure employment or, at very least, entry to a lodge abroad. On arrival at their destination they could expect support in the form of advice and assistance in finding employment, long-term accommodation and local information from fellow Masons. The initiation fee was welcomed in depressed and shrinking communities and travel was facilitated. A letter from the Freemason's Secretary of the Lodge of Probity in Halifax, Yorkshire in 1816 refers to:

> a Tramp came to be relieved by my workmen and I recollected having seen him there about six months before, on the same errand. He informed me that he had travelled since the time he was here before, nearly all over the Kingdom, also Ireland and part of Scotland and he had saved money by it as he was an Orangeman and an Oddfellow. He had been relieved by them and he meant to be made a Mason when he got home, which was in the neighbourhood of Stockport.

Travelling certificates sometimes included a physical description. After 1813 all Master Mason certificates issued by UGLE gave the lodge name and date of initiation using both the Gregorian Calendar, i.e. the dating system in common use, and the Masonic one, AL or *anno lucis* (in the year of light). This dating system is equivalent to the Gregorian year plus 4,000. For example, AD 1717, the year Grand Lodge was formed, would become 5717 AL. The original Grand Lodge certificates from 1755 until 1819 had been in English only. The Antients' Grand Lodge had issued certificates in English and Latin from 1766. In 1819 UGLE started producing certificates in both languages. Until 1963 the certificates were in both Latin and English. In January 1965 United Grand Lodge of England omitted Latin from Grand Lodge certificates.

Across the Empire local Hindu, Muslim, Sikh and Parsi men sought to mingle with their colonial counterparts without religious or cultural barriers. Those who were unable to advance outside the lodge could gain status as Masters within it. As a unified British structure was not created, bear in mind that your ancestor might have joined a Grand Lodge from a country other than that you expected. If he had lived in Hong Kong he might have joined a Masonic lodge associated with the Grand Lodge of Scotland or one within the

United Grand Lodge England or one linked to the Grand Lodge of Ireland. All of those bodies had lodges there and a Grand Lodge of China also exists, based in Taipei. When searching have to hand the occupation, the known locations and the dates of the life of your ancestor. Freemason and author Rudyard Kipling, 1865–1936, explained that he was Entered for membership by a Hindu, Passed by a Mohammedan and Raised by an Englishman. The Tyler was an Indian Jew. This is reflected in his 1895 poem, 'The Mother Lodge'.

> Outside – 'Sergeant! Sir! Salute! Salaam!'
> Inside – 'Brother, an' it doesn't do no 'arm.
> We met upon the Level an' we parted on the Square,
> An' I was junior Deacon in my Mother-Lodge out there!'

The Cama family migrated from Persia to the Surat area of India in the eighteenth century and established a vast trading empire. Its members joined lodges where they met colonial merchants from France and England and in 1855 established the first Indian business in the City of London. Members of the family progressed within Freemasonry and were attracted to the Order of the Secret Monitor in England and India. Honour and trust in business deals may have been strengthened by the relationships they built in the lodges. Studies based on directors of companies listed at the London Stock Exchange and in census returns between 1861 and 1901 have identified 16 per cent as Freemasons.

WOMEN FREEMASONS

There was also a growth in Freemasonry among women. Co-Freemasonry which admits both men and women began in France in the 1890s with the forming of *Le Droit Humain*. In 1902 French lodges for women and men were opened in England. The largest British Masonic Order admitting women, the Honourable Fraternity of Antient Masonry, http://www.hfaf.org/, 402 Finchley Road, Childs Hill, London, NW2 2HR, was founded in 1908. It campaigned for votes for women (for the first time some women over 30 could vote in the General Election of 1918). In 1916 it aided the establishment of the Halsey Training College to train secondary school teachers and subsequently the establishment of a Bureau of Service. Having been dominated by aristocratic women prior to the First World War, it became more middle class after the First World War. In 1935 it became formally a single-sex organisation and in 1958 it became the Order of Women Freemasons. There are extensive minute books of Grand Lodge and of the Board of General Purposes and of some of the individual lodges. Lodge Mercury, No. 11, was consecrated in 1928 and was a 'travelling' lodge which toured the country initiating members in various provincial centres until there were sufficient core members in each place to form their own lodge. Apart from minute books and Treasurers' books, the archive at Headquarters holds surrendered warrants and a miscellaneous collection of agendas and other lodge papers, such as Gentlemen's Night programmes. Since 2000, the agendas of the lodges meeting at Headquarters are put on CD. Photographs of the two Golden and Diamond Jubilee celebrations at the Royal Albert Hall are held in the archive, together with the slides of the Diamond Jubilee Pageant. To these are now added the DVD and associated material from the centenary meeting at the Royal Albert Hall in June 2008. There is also material on the Honourable Fraternity of the Antient Masonry in the archive of the British Federation of International Co-Freemasonry, in the periodical of the Honourable Fraternity of Antient Masonry, the *Gavel*, the *Co-Mason*, the journal of *Le Droit Humain* and the suffrage periodicals – the *Vote, Votes for Women* and the *Common Cause*. There are no digitalised records of either the Honourable Fraternity of Antient Masonry or the Order of Women Freemasons.

TWENTIETH CENTURY

Between 1874, when the Prince of Wales was elected as Grand Master of the UGLE, and 1901 the number of lodges doubled from 1,400 to 2,800. In 1901 King Edward VII called himself the 'Protector of English Freemasonry' and announced that he intended to rejoice in the prosperity and growth of Freemasonry. Although counting the number of Freemasons is difficult, as many Masons join more than one lodge, it is clear that throughout most of the twentieth century the number of lodges grew. Sometimes this followed specific legislation, such as the Shops Act of 1911 which introduced statutory holidays for staff. Several new lodges met on the half day when shops were shut and attracted retailers, tradesmen and their employees. During and immediately following the First World War there was a growth spurt. The number of Grand Lodge certificates issued to new Master Masons rose from 13,352 in 1914 to 30,983 in 1921. Membership doubled between 1917 and 1929. In 1928 *The Times* estimated that there were 462,000 members (322,000 Masons in lodges affiliated to United Grand Lodge England, an Irish membership of 50,000 and a Scottish one of 90,000). In 1938 *The Times* explained the interwar expansion as being due to the continued interest of the royal family and the proliferation of specialist lodges, particularly those focused on former pupils at specific public schools.

In the 1930s and 1940s Freemasons were persecuted in (among other places) Nazi Germany, Vichy France, Mussolini's Italy and in all countries dominated by Stalin. In Britain the disincentive to membership was often economic. Weedon's account of the London-based lodge, *History of the Lodge of St John No. 1370, 1870–1953*, indicates that the initiation fee in 1919 was 15 guineas. There was also an annual subscription of 4 guineas and members would be expected to give to charity and attend, with a guest, at least some of the meals at Restaurant Frascati, which involved paying a dining fee. There was an annual Ladies' Festival, which in 1923 cost a guinea per person, and again a member would be expected to bring guests. Masons were

This Masonic Craft Officer's collar is on display in the open-air museum at Beamish. Located between Durham and Newcastle, the museum includes a Masonic hall set in 1913. Originally built by St John's Lodge of Sunderland in 1869–70, the Masons left in the 1930s. Some of the building was moved to the museum and there was extensive reconstruction to make it appear as it probably did in 1913. It opened to the public in 2006. (© Brian Snelson)

expected to wear smart suits and regalia and there would have been travel costs incurred for those attending meetings. In 1934 workers at Ford's, Dagenham, earned £4 a week, those in the potteries received less and miners took home less than £3. On the other hand, in times of economic uncertainty making opportunities to network might have been seen as of importance. Membership grew and between 1909 and 1939 the national press carried over 200 reports on the consecration of new lodges. The Second World War saw a boost in membership in both the armed forces and among prisoners of war. This growth continued after the war. There were 47 new UGLE lodges in 1938 and 190 in 1946. The net increase in lodges in the period 1946–55 was over 1,000. It took 220 years to establish the first 6,000 lodges and another 4,000 were added after 1938.

As prosperity spread so the social class of the membership did. Nevertheless, the 1960s and 1970s saw a period of decline from the previous high levels of membership. Possibly family life and socialising with spouses became more popular, possibly other forms of entertainment, notably television, attracted people in ways which lodge meetings did not. Although Freemasonry is not a religion and is open to members of many religions, for its adherents it can be a spiritual journey and this was a time when there were widespread challenges to religion and a decline in church attendance. This was also a period that saw both friendly societies and Freemasons reduce their use of banners and regalia on municipal parades. In the case of the former this was in part because of their focus on providing healthcare or mortgage services while the latter ceased to have a high public profile during a century when it was condemned by the Vatican and there was persecution of Freemasons by the Nazis and in the USSR. Freemasonry may well have continued to be attractive because it provided opportunities for self-development. Lodges created records, notably minute, signature and account books, which were similar to those used in many businesses. The posts of Treasurer, Secretary and Almoner were elected and older members were able to mentor, develop or train younger ones, enabling them to engender trustworthiness and administrative and social skills. However, during the twentieth century opportunities to learn these skills outside the lodge increased. While more working-class men joined, they often expressed concern about the costs. Lodges started to move away from expensive areas. Royal Jubilee Lodge and Balham Lodge moved from central London to Middlesex, in 1990 and Surrey, in 1993. The number of ladies' nights with expensive gifts for guests declined and there was less interest in the sort of structured comradeship that men had found attractive in the past. *Freemasonry and the Press in the Twentieth Century. A National Newspaper Study of England and Wales* (2013) by Paul Calderwood, a former journalist who then wrote a doctoral thesis on the topic, concluded that from the beginning of the twentieth century until the 1960s 'approximately seven-eighths' of national (i.e. almost always London-based) press coverage of freemasonry was laudatory. The tone of coverage then changed. Freemasonry declined in popularity, Freemasons appeared less frequently in their regalia on processions and there were more references made that associated it with conspiracy and favouritism.

The Times' estimation of membership in 1985 was 500,000, then 300,000 by 1995 with funds of over £300 million. In 1996 UGLE told a Committee of the Commons that it had fewer than 350,000 members. In 1998 only 10,815 new Grand Lodge certificates were issued. In 2005 UGLE announced that there were 320,000 members in 8,661 lodges. The Freemasons suffered reputational damage. An Italian lodge, P2, was closed in 1976 after it became associated with the Mafia and the Vatican. In Britain senior politicians demanded that the links between the police and the Freemasons be broken. A parliamentary committee investigated the role of Freemasons in public life in 1999. In the same year, the Welsh Assembly placed a legal requirement on membership declaration for Freemasons. In July 2001 the European Court of Human Rights confirmed that 'Freemasonry was neither a secret, criminal nor an illegal organization'. However, by this point English Freemasonry was being accused of cronyism and of obstructing parliamentary processes. In 2002 the press reported that Rowan Williams, the Archbishop of Canterbury, had expressed reservations about Freemasonry's secrets, rituals and its 'mutual back-scratching'. Although he later said that his views had been misrepresented, he reaffirmed his 'personal unease' about Freemasonry. In response, UGLE has frequently reiterated that membership involves service to others rather than being self-serving and that the prime and inalienable qualification for admission into its lodges is a belief in God. The Home Secretary demanded that the UGLE hand over a list of all members in the judiciary or the police. UGLE refused, but a voluntary register was created. The Association of Women Barristers demanded that judges who were Freemasons should declare this and legislation was passed to force the judiciary to declare if they were Freemasons. Although Masonic rules state that it is a misuse of membership to expect material gain for themselves or others, this has not been widely reported. In March 2008 the *Daily Mail* stated: 'Masons are widely believed to further the business and professional interests of brother Masons, although they would deny this and claim it is a harmless social and charitable organisation.'

In 2018, after the *Guardian* reported that clandestine lodges existed for politicians and journalists, the UGLE placed advertisements in major newspapers stating that Freemasonry was a fraternal organisation with charitable aims which had raised £33 million pounds in 2017. The UGLE argued that its members had been misrepresented and stigmatised and it complained to the Equality and Human Rights Commission. The lodges in question were not secret, being the subject of Wikipedia entries, published histories and an article in *Labour History Review*. The place and dates of meetings can be found in the annual publication, *Directory of Lodges and Chapters*. Nevertheless, the National Union of Journalists and a Tory MP called for the registration of Freemasons.

Although a *Guardian* journalist argued, 'No one joins the masons for the handshakes. It must be for the benefits it can bring', studies of Freemasons and their personal testimony suggest that many are attracted to the ritual, the traditions and the philanthropic activity. For example, Scott Kenney's recent study of Masons in Canada, *Brought to Light: Contemporary Freemasonry, Meaning, and Society* (2016), found that men joined and remained for much the same reasons as your ancestors might have done. These included wanting to form friendships and make sense of the world, because of curiosity about Masonry's secrets and often because a family member was a Mason. The lodge was seen as a safe environment in which to gain new skills, where members felt encouraged to learn, to be tolerant and to be charitable. Even if you cannot record your own ancestor (there is advice about recording people's memories in Chapter 2), you can gain a sense of what Freemasonry meant to people from their descendants. Listening to one or two recordings may help you to consider what questions you would like to ask. The British Library holds one of the largest collections of oral history and life-story interviews in the world. Included are recordings of Freemasons and also of recollections of Freemasons. Alan Carr was born in 1936 in London and was recorded when aged about 60. You can hear the interview at: https://sounds.bl.uk/Oral-history/ Law/021M-C0736 X0002XX-0001V0, and there is also a transcript. Alan's father was a Freemason from about 1929 until his death in 1983. Alan recalled that his father became a historian of Freemasonry and that 'he went round the world, he went to Iran and Australia and the States and everywhere talking to people about the subject. He was very much invited to do it, and he was editing a journal, a research journal on it'. Once you know this about Alan's father you can look for further evidence online. There is an example of Harry Carr's work at: https://www.scribd.com/document/193729820/AQC-H-Carr-Kipling-the-Craft-pdf. Alan Carr went on:

> there used to be a certain amount of dressing up. I know very little about Freemasonry. I remember seeing photographs of him in Masonic regalia. I remember him and my mother going to ladies' nights in London hotels in the sort of Fifties and Sixties, and later than that too. It was sort of to some extent a sort of glamorous part of life.

Personal testimony indicates that Freemasonry has attracted people from all walks of life because it has been relatively inclusive. Its principles of brotherly love, relief and truth are supposed to be applied irrespective of members' backgrounds or views regarding religion or politics. The money that Freemasons raise for charity is from their own efforts, they do not ask others to donate. They argue that they seek to promote confidence and to make members into better citizens.

Freemasonry may have helped to foster Enlightenment ideals and assisted in the emergence of civil society and facilitated education but, being highly organised, with lodges managing their own matters, overseen by provincial and national lodges, it can appear bureaucratic. Those prized roles within Freemasonry are seen as of less significance in the twenty-first century. Other bodies perform some of its tasks. Its social service and insurance functions have been replaced and many lodges are dominated by older men. The Empire and the army, once of importance to Freemasonry, have diminished. However, it continues to offer an oath-bound, safe space for ritual and social bonding, to engage in charitable work. Religion is not discussed in the lodge but through Freemasonry some members are able to build relevant meanings for themselves and to make sense of a perplexing world. While Freemasonry might be resistant to change and struggling to find itself, it is clear that some lodges mentor and encourage learning through engagement in activities and offer moral and ethical benefits. Studies suggest that long-term retention within a lodge correlates with efficient, tactful organisation, the existence of close ties between members and a sense of good fellowship and support. This might not seem of direct relevance to your studies of the past, but an understanding of the present can inform how we perceive the past and the actions of ancestors who were Freemasons.

Chapter 6

FRIENDLY SOCIETIES

Friendly societies were established to assist members, and sometimes others, financially in time of illness, old age and hardship. Often members paid into a box (and they have also been called box clubs), usually secured with three locks so that it could only be opened when three keyholders were present. Members received funding from the box in the event of being unable to work at their normal trade. Payments were also made to their widows on their death. Members often met in pubs and the societies offered sociability, through drinking and feasting; public demonstrations of fraternity, on parades and at funerals; and private affirmations of solidarity, through visiting the sick. Most friendly societies were run by their members, who elected the officers. The larger societies developed branches, often called lodges, and sometimes Tents or Courts, around the world.

Beyond the notion of facilitating risk-sharing among members through the organised transfer of money, a wide variety of structures were created. Their focus has not always been only mutual saving. Some were emphatically local, others based on trades or religious affiliation. Some sought to protect and further the wider rights and interests of their members. Few of these clubs remained solvent for long and often they had to increase the qualifying period of time before new members could receive benefits or had to close the box for several months. Sometimes members were driven out of the societies. Some of those clubs that invested their funds (for example, in bonds or property) had financial management problems. Until the nineteenth century when there were disputes between members some law courts were unwilling to accept the cases due to uncertainty of the legal standing of societies. Since the 1990s many have merged or closed. There is a list of many of these on the website of the trade body that represents mutual and not-for-profit insurers, friendly societies and other financial mutuals across the UK, the Association of Financial Mutuals, http://www.financialmutuals.org/members/tracing-a-society.

This chapter provides an account of friendly societies using significant legislation in the 1790s, 1911 and the 1940s as divisions. It also outlines some sources which are specific to friendly societies. There is an account of a social event, recollections of charitable activity and rituals and, in recognition of how friendly societies have been used as vehicles for a variety of other activities, there is a note about links to Chartism.

THE LONG NINETEENTH CENTURY

In 1769 a local Act established friendly societies in every Devon parish, but the payments made were so generous that the pressure on the rates was deemed to be too high and in 1773 the legislation was repealed. Within the upper class a consensus emerged that a statutory framework was required. Friendly societies were seen as a solution to the widespread rural poverty of the period. They were also seen as a useful way to promote the values of hard work and discipline. Furthermore, following the 1789 revolution in France, there were also increased fears of strikes and radical activity by trade-focused clubs. The Friendly Societies Act, 1793 regulated and supported those societies which registered their rules at quarter sessions. Since the 1660s in order to be able to claim poor relief, that is a payment from the local authorities if you were destitute, people needed to be able to prove that they were members of the parish. A settlement certificate gave the right of a person to live and receive welfare in their parish of legal settlement. This might not be the parish of their birth. Certificates were issued by the Overseer of the

Poor. This person was responsible to the vestry, was elected annually and had other duties. Under the 1793 Act friendly society members could gain exemption from legal settlement if they could obtain a certificate signed and witnessed by two officers of the society. A Justice of the Peace, JP, had to endorse the certificate. Examples of this sort of certificate exist in many local record offices. They indicate the status of friendly societies and a way in which they promoted helped to control the supply of labour. Friendly society rules, once submitted, could be subject to amendment by a JP. Further minor amendments to the law were made in 1795. Many societies did not register, either because they wished to avoid magisterial control or because of the expense of appearing before the Clerk of the Peace in the county town. Nevertheless, registrations and the 1803–4 returns of local clubs by Overseers of the Poor resulted in large amounts of information which might be of interest to family historians.

Although members were not supposed to reveal the rituals of fraternal bodies, they could own rule books and reminders as to the rituals and you might well find examples of these in a box in the garage, in museums or available for sale online. The rules confirmed by Justices of the Peace indicate the values and ideas of the societies. There are rules about the number of members and excluding those in dangerous trades or who were poorly paid. There were clubs for women and many of these had rules against specific jobs or against women with husbands in dangerous trades. Many societies insisted that members be Protestant and British. Some clubs excluded through high admission fees and subscriptions. Beyond core benefits, sickness and death of the member, some made payments for the death of a spouse, or in cases of imprisonment, old age or pregnancy. Sometimes the names of members as well as officers were recorded and preserved. There were a series of subsequent Acts regulating the societies.

RULE BOOKS

The National Records of Scotland holds rules and regulations and statements of constitution of friendly societies and trade unions, 1632–1971, held in FS1-14. These include the Kilmarnock Coal Cutters Society (FS1/2/41) and the Carfin Colliery Friendly Society (FS1/16/29). Collections of rule books can be found in The National Archives. There are some in the British Library where you can find the Rules and Regulations of the Enginemen's Union Fund (Newcastle upon Tyne), 1822, the Articles, Rules, and Orders of the Friendly Society, held at the house of Mrs Mary Gardner, Chowdean Fell (Gateshead), 1828 and the Rules, Orders, and Regulations, of a Friendly Society of Women (of Spalding, Lincolnshire), 1808. There are also examples in many county record offices. For example, Leicestershire Record Office has the following items: Nottingham Oddfellows Friendly Society, Ceremonials of the Minor Lodges, 1843; Appleby Old Friendly Society, Ledger; Women's Friendly Society, Belgrave, Articles manuscript, the Rules, Orders, and Regulations of a Friendly Society Established 3 June 1773 at the Bell, of Morcott, 1821; the Minute Books of the Leicester Bond Street Friendly Society and the Nottingham Ancient Imperial Unity of Oddfellows, Triumph Lodge (Lubenham) and the Account Book, Glenfield Female Friendly Society. To find county record offices, see: http://discovery.nationalarchives.gov.uk/find-an-archive. There are reports on numerous societies in The National Archives, Kew. These are, as Audrey Fisk noted in her study of the Ancient Order of Foresters, *Mutual self-help in Southern England 1850–1912* (2006), a 'seemingly under-utilised resource'. The National Register of Archives and Access to Archives are both available via The National Archives website: http://www.nationalarchives.gov.uk. There are papers relating to the friendly society membership of individuals included in the archives of other organisations. These can be found via the Archives Hub search engine at: http://

archiveshub.ac.uk/. The National Archives collates data about new accessions from archives in Britain and Ireland, http://www.nationalarchives.gov.uk/accessions/. This information appears in its catalogue at: http://discovery.nationalarchives.gov.uk. There are also a few rule books in the International Institute for Social History, in Amsterdam. You can request that items are ready for when you visit via its website at: https://socialhistory.org.

This sash was on display in the Britannia Panopticon, Glasgow in 2010. The records of the Independent Order of Rechabites, Salford Unity, Friendly Society (IOR), a teetotal friendly society for women and men founded in Salford in 1835, are held largely in Glasgow and London. The IOR spread across the UK and to New Zealand, Australia, the USA and India and still exists today. Its archives include national, district and local minutes, journals and directories, conference reports and papers, books and case files. It came to Scotland in 1837, and the Dumfries and Edinburgh Tents were founded in 1838. The Edinburgh area was its first District. By 1841 there were 47 Scottish Tents and 4,000 Rechabites. It is ironic that the sash ended up in the music hall as the rules state that the 'singing of indecent songs' during meetings was expressly prohibited. (© Alan J. Stuart)

One way that friendly societies could reduce risk was to join affiliated societies. These were regional, later national or international 'Orders', such as the Ancient Order of Foresters which emerged in the early nineteenth century and which authorised the creation of semi-autonomous local branches. The AoF branches were called Courts and the chair was the Chief Ranger. In 1847 most of the Foresters' seventy-five Courts in Liverpool had to close due to a cholera epidemic. In order to aid recovery the organisation made a loan to the district. This was not repaid.

Similarly, elaborate titles were employed by the other Orders. The Independent Order of Oddfellows, Manchester Unity was one of the largest of the friendly societies. There are records of many of these activities in local record offices. The records of the Oddfellows King William IV Lodge, Lancaster, are held at the County Archives in Preston. In 1861 William Huddlestone was fined 5*s.* for drunkenness while claiming 'on the box'. However, because he had a wife and several young children he was allowed to keep his sick pay of 9*s.* When James Richardson was arrested for drunkenness his wife rushed to the shop of the appropriate Oddfellow official, Edward Gardner, so that he could be declared well and thus avoid a fine and the stopping of sick pay. The fine was remitted but the family lost the sick pay. In 1866 the Preston District allowed a £5 benefit to a widow with seven children who was not entitled as her husband had been suspended from membership at the time of his death.

Similar accounts can be found in the records held in the record office, Coventry. The Oddfellows Philanthropic Lodge, Coventry, expelled Henry Hollis after he was convicted of robbery. However, Hollis appealed and eighty-one members attended a meeting to hear his case. If he was expelled he would be unable to access any money that he had contributed and may have been ineligible to join another society on grounds of age. He stated that he had not stolen the society's beer, but only helped to drink it and that he had been punished: 'I have been in the lodge for many years and am now getting old. I hope and trust you will do what is right by me and take me again into the lodge as I suffered imprisonment for the whole of the workmen who drank the beer.' The lodge agreed to reinstate him but this was overturned by the District. In 1875 Henry Aires of the same lodge was spotted by the Noble Grand (the elected chair of the lodge) working while in receipt of sick pay. When reminded of the rules, Aires broke another rule by using insulting and abusive language. He was expelled but on appeal to the District and then to Grand Master his sentence was reduced to suspension for a year.

When checking the indexes and contents of local record offices bear in mind that record offices sometimes hold cash books, membership lists, application forms and information relating to meeting places. From 1793 there was the deposit with magistrates of financial bonds for officers who handled money. Bonds can be found in the county record offices. Sometimes the money was invested and the names, addresses and occupations of those with responsibility for this activity also had to be supplied to the JP. For example, in 1805 John Scott, John Hinckley and John Doll, a rope maker, a boat builder and a leather dresser respectively, all of Bermondsey, deposited a bond of £200 on behalf of the Friends to Peace Friendly Society of Southwark. In 1806 the same JP received a £30 bond for Ann Aubertin, spinster and Secretary, Peter Aubertin, Clerk, and Daniel Lambert, Gentleman, who represented the Banstead and Chipstead Female Benefit Society. As was typical, the men's society met in the pub, in this case The Ship in Southwark, while the women met in the Sunday school room, Banstead, and were regulated by men. Sometimes a bond was drawn up between the publican and the officers of a society. Such an arrangement was made between Charles Palmer, landlord of The Rose, Bermondsey, and his partner, Robert Campion, and two Stewards of the Southwark Assurance Friendly Society, William Simmonds and Simon Wale. When Daniel Swallow, landlord of The King and Queen, Rotherhithe, went bankrupt in 1801 the Royal Oak Benefit Society transferred its allegiances, and its box, to The Boatswain and

Pall. A bond document was drawn up and it includes a list of forty-seven society members.

During the nineteenth century the incentives for friendly societies to register with the government increased. Friendly societies were exempt from some taxation and could sue for stolen funds (a common problem) if they provided a set of their rules for the local JPs. After 1817 registered societies were permitted to deposit their funds in savings banks at favourable interest rates. In 1818 further legislation meant that all rules and tables of payments to be made to both the society by members and to members, when ill, by the society, should be checked and approved by JPs. Many JPs accepted the word of local schoolmasters and others who had no real knowledge of the technical difficulties and many unsound societies continued to exist, but the intention was clear. It was the desire to reduce the rates as the poor, and particularly the ill poor, were perceived to be a burden on the rates. Ratepayers could receive rates-funded assistance with pensions or funeral expenses and friendly society arrears could be paid from the rates in order to stop people becoming more of a burden on the rates.

The extent of the survival of records varies. Many societies have disappeared, their records lost. Even societies that survive have not got complete sets of records which are likely to be of interest to family historians. Moreover, records were rarely kept in one central location. Some of the larger friendly societies (the Affiliated Orders) had local branches. The affiliated Orders collected and published information about membership, financial value, sickness data, average ages of members, where and when lodges (or Courts) met and names of officials. In the case of the Ancient Order of Foresters, founded in 1834, records were grouped into Districts. When a member died this was reported to the District and then the money for the funeral expenses was paid. Districts published mortality lists in conjunction with their quarterly accounts. Some list date of birth of the member, his date of joining, date of marriage, first name of wife (the Foresters was open only to men until the 1890s) and date

Registered No. 3918.

NINETY-FIFTH
HALF-YEARLY REPORT

OF THE

SMALLBRIDGE EQUITABLE

Sick & Burial Society,

HELD AT

GARSIDE CHAMBERS,

GARSIDE STREET,

SMALLBRIDGE.

From June 18th, to December 31st 1907.

Number of Members, 470.

The Next Half-Yearly Meeting will be held on Tuesday Evening, July 7th, 1908, at 7-30 p.m.

Members are particularly required to observe the following Rules.

That any Member receiving sick pay being from home after Six o'clock at night in the Winter Months, and Nine o'clock at night in the Summer Months, or going more than Three miles from his place of abode, without the consent of the Steward, shall be fined 2s. 6d., from the 1st of October to the 31st March, to be considered the Winter Months, and from the 1st of April to the 30th of September, the Summer Months. *See Rule 18.*

That all arrears be deducted out of the first payment made to any member, whether it be a sick or funeral allowance.

If any member neglects to pay his contributions for six months, he shall be no longer a member of this society.

That every member pay the whole of his arrears every six months, or in default thereof he shall be fined twopence, such fine if not paid within six months will exclude him from sick benefits until such time as the fine be paid.

See Rules 17, 20, and 21.

Resolution passed at the half-yearly Meeting June 18th, 1901.

That all Members who require to avail themselves of the Sick Fund must give Notice to the Stewards before 2 o'clock p.m. on the day of Notice, or the week will not commence until the day following.

J. Dawson & Son, Printers, Halifax Road, Rochdale.

The 1907 Smallbridge Sick and Burial Society Half-Yearly Report has the names of the officers and the names, occupations, addresses and ages of those who had applied to become members since the last report. It listed the 'Sick Stewards' for each of the four Districts covered by the society, giving their addresses and the areas they covered. There were balance sheets and the names of recipients of sick pay and the sums received. There was also a list of the eight funerals for the period covered. These included three women. On the back page there was a reminder to members of three important rules. (Author's collection)

and cause of death. Some from those parts of the country that ran widows and orphans schemes include the birth dates of children registered for benefits. The records in other parts of the country have been lost or destroyed and some of the surviving records only mention the date of death of a member. In order to join a man had to be introduced by two members. They were often relations and there are records of some of these men. Moreover, members, at least

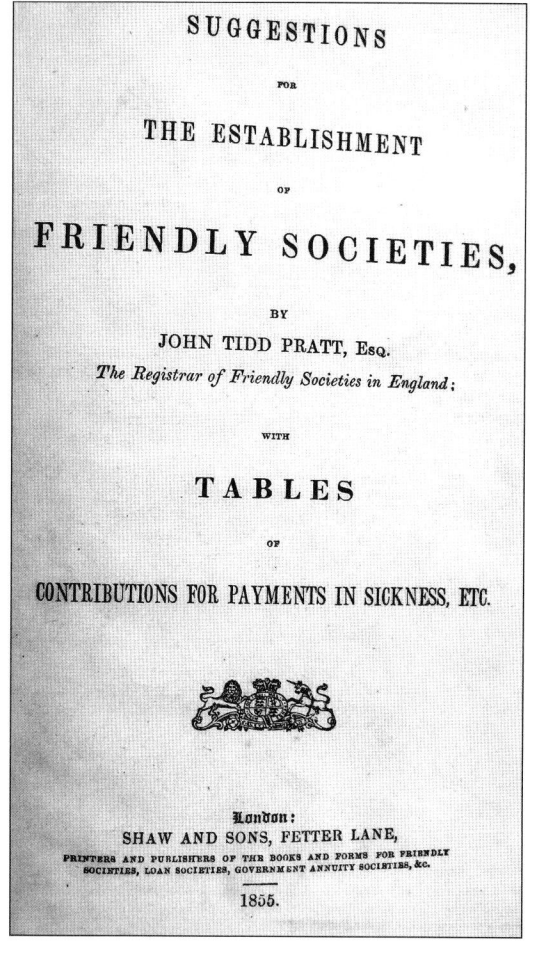

John Tidd Pratt, 1797–1870 was, as it notes on this publication, the Registrar of Friendly Societies of England. He also wrote a history of savings banks and as a barrister was counsel to certify the rules of savings banks and friendly societies, 1834–46. (Author's collection)

initially, had to live within 2½ miles of where the Court (branch) met. This was almost always a pub.

The future of the Foresters Heritage Trust Museum & Archive in Southampton is uncertain and it may not be open at the time of publication. For details about which Ancient Order of Foresters records survive you should contact the Ancient Order of Foresters Heritage Trust, a voluntary independent registered charity, governed by eight trustees and located in Southampton; email: enquiries@ aoforestersheritage.com.

The AoF directory of 1867 contained information about 3,600 Courts and Oddfellows directory has similar data. On the AoF see Audrey Fisk and Roger Logan's *Grandfather was in the Foresters* (1994) and Roger Logan's *An introduction to friendly society records* (2000).

The Foresters' directory for 1890 listed 1,436 juvenile societies with 85,125 members, and by 1900 there were 125,274. The names and addresses of juvenile society Secretaries are listed, as are the details of Court Secretaries. Recruiting children to the societies gave the AoF a more family focus. There were sports and competitions and a variety of roles for adults. Other societies also sought to attract young people. In 1902, according to its directory, the Oddfellows had 1,662 juvenile societies with 111,512 members. Part of the reason for this interest in younger members might have been because, from about 1870, there is evidence that people were living longer. James C. Riley's study, *Sick, Not Dead: The Health of British Workingmen during the Mortality Decline* (1997) is based on AoF friendly society records. Riley suggests that as they got older, people tended to report more illness. Some members began to access additional treatment and medicines through the Friendly Society Medical Association. Dispensary addresses and details and the names and addresses of Secretaries and Medical Officers began to be included in AoF directories from 1874.

If an Affiliated Order friendly society member was paid up-to-date he could receive a 'clearance certificate' from his lodge which could be presented to another lodge. This could include overseas travel. Some chose to retain membership of their mother lodge. They empowered their new local lodge to act as an agent and report when the member was entitled to draw on funds. This could operate across thousands of miles. In Norfolk the Loyal Trafalgar Lodge of Oddfellows granted 'clearance' to Brother Henry Hollis when he went to America and it made a sick payment to Brother Ward, who, although 'residing in Australia', had maintained his membership. If your ancestor was in an Affiliated Order then his name might appear in records of his mother lodge long after he left the area. In 1842 alone, the Independent Order of Oddfellows Manchester Unity paid out £5,200 to migrant workers and during the ten years between 1863 and 1872 the number of individual payments amounted to well over £90,000.

There are other examples of societies with existing records of members. There is information about the names, occupations, ages and addresses of 871 members of the West Suffolk Society, 1830–72. Records of the Royal Berkshire Friendly Society, 1872–1972 can be found in Berkshire Record Office. There were also similar societies. Starting with the Great Western Railway Provident Society, created in 1838, railway companies established friendly societies. Membership was compulsory and, as it provided sickness and retirement benefits, it undermined the prospects for any independent workers' organisations. There was also interest in another fraternal body. The directors of the Great Eastern Railway Company paid for two Masonic meeting rooms to be incorporated into the Great Eastern Hotel opened at Liverpool Street in 1884. Wyndham S. Portal used the Hampshire Friendly Society (of which he was a trustee) as model when he, as deputy chair of the company, established a friendly society for workers of the London and South Western Railway. Firemen and drivers on the North Eastern formed their own society, but still requested funding from their employer. By 1870 there were around eighty railway friendly societies.

There are many accounts of specific societies, and these include books produced by the societies themselves, such as the following:

Mary Bliss and Mary Day, *Cirencester Benefit Society 1890–1990* (1990).
Richardson Campbell, *Rechabite history; a record of the origin, rise, and progress of the Independent Order of Rechabites, Salford Unity from its institution on August 25th, 1835, to the present time* (1911).

Daniel Herbert Roper and John Harrison, *The First Hundred Years: 1868–1968: the Story of the National Deposit Friendly Society* (1968).

Ian Saddler, *A mission in life. The History of Liverpool Victoria Friendly Society* (1997).

Sometimes societies produce souvenir histories such as the Nottingham Oddfellows Friendly Society's 175th Anniversary Souvenir Booklet or David Tregoning and Hugh Cockerell's account of a society founded by Quakers in Yorkshire, *Friends for Life. Friends' Provident Life Office 1832–1882* (1982). A further example is Harold F. Buss and R.G. Burnett's *A Goodly Fellowship: A History of the Hundred Years of the Methodist Local Preachers Mutual Aid Association, 1849–1949* (1949). A good source for such books as these are online auctions or booksellers.

It is also sensible to lookout for accounts by local historians. These often appear in local history magazines or are distributed in only a small area. These examples are all from the twentieth century but there are plenty from the more recent period:

Revd J.M.J. Fletcher, 'Some Records of an Eighteenth Century Benefit Society', *Derbyshire Archaeological and Natural History Society Journal*, Vol. 33, 1911.

Herbert J.M. Maltby, 'Early Manchester and Salford Friendly Societies', *Transactions of the Lancashire and Cheshire Antiquarian Society*, 46, 1929.

G.W. Martin, 'Two Early Friendly Societies in Essex', *Essex Countryside*, 13, 1965.

Laurence Marriott Wulcko, *Some Early Friendly Societies in Buckinghamshire* (1951).

In the twenty-first century, *Local Historian* magazine has carried material on friendly societies such as Robert Humphreys' 'The development of friendly societies in nineteenth-century Surrey' (35, 3 August 2005), http://www.balh.org.uk/publications/local-historian/

the-local-historian-volume-35-number-3-august-2005, and Mavis Curtis' analyses of a society established in 1808 in Marsden, near Huddersfield, 'An early nineteenth-century women's friendly society in Yorkshire' (46, 2, April 2016), http://www.balh.org.uk/ publications /local-historian/the-local-historian-volume-46-number-2-april-2016. Copies of *Local Historian* are held in many local record offices and libraries.

There are also scholarly accounts of societies in specific areas. Here are some of the many examples:

>Margaret Fuller, *West Country Friendly Societies: An Account of Village Benefit Clubs and their Brass Pole Heads* (1964).
>Hilary Marland, *Medicine and Society in Wakefield and Huddersfield, 1780–1870* (1987).
>David Neave, *Feasts, Fellowship, and Financial Aid: South Holderness Friendly Societies* (1986).
>David Neave, *Mutual Aid in the Victorian Countryside: Friendly Societies in the Rural East Riding* (1991).

A FEAST DAY OUTING TO MONMOUTH, 1828
The below account from *Odd Fellows Magazine* indicates that whatever occurred on the trip, the record was of an event that was seemly and joyous. This is conveyed by the elevated language ('The tinkling strings of the harp now summoned the votaries of Terpsichore to the pleasures of the mazy dance') and the reminders of the image of Oddfellowship as respectable. Within the space of the first sentence the Oddfellows both declares itself independent and also refers to the patronage of a duke. The support of the Church is implied by the reference to the merry bells and later the author makes clear that although the Headquarters for the day was a pub, the first thing that the members did on arrival was to be 'unanimous' in their admiration of the castle. It is probable that the 'foreign weed' was the respectable drug of the period: tobacco.

The Waterloo lodge of the Independent Odd Fellows made their annual summer excursion on Monday the 4th [of August] within the celebrated ruins of Ragland Castle, eight miles distant therefrom, the use thereof being kindly granted to them by A. Wyatt Esq. agent of the Duke of Beaufort. The preparations for the occasion were conducted with the same spirit-stirring zeal which has ever marked the proceedings of the Waterloo lodge. At six o'clock the merry bells of St Mary's tower proclaimed, in clamour loud, the commencement of this Odd Fellows' holiday. A little before nine, the full band marched up to the lodge house, in the street leading from which to the river the conveyances took their ground. The signal for starting off being given, the procession moved off, headed by the band with two cars and led by the Grand Master of the district in an open chariot-and-four followed by six other chariots, whilst the rear was made up of gigs, cars etc. making an aggregate of twenty five conveyances on its entry into Ragland, besides numerous horsemen, pedestrians etc. At the village of Mitchelltry the inhabitants had erected an arch of flowers and their example was followed at the turn-pike gate near Thloft-y-thloi and a third rose in its arial bow at the top of the hill leading into Ragland. The brethren and their friends dismounted at the Beaufort Arms Inn (the headquarters for the day) and immediately repaired to the Castle, in the Yellow Tower of which floated the Union Jack. Unanimous was the feeling of admiration on the survey of these far-famed remains of castellated splendour. After a cursory glance and slight refreshment being partaken of, a procession was formed on the terrace in front of the entrance gateway and eighty-four brethren walked in full costume with the insignia of the Order through the village returning to the castle in the same order amid the assembled crowds that lined the road. At two o'clock dinner was announced to which

> nearly 200 sat down under a large tent in the Fountain Court. The cloth being removed the usual routine of toasts were given and the pleasures of the evening were enlivened by some excellent singing and recitations composed for the occasion. The tinkling strings of the harp now summoned the votaries of Terpsichore to the pleasures of the mazy dance and two parties were soon formed on the bowling green to enjoy this, their favourite amusement. The Castle, at this time presented the most animated appearance to the dancers on the green, tea parties in the tent, the porter's lodge crowded with an attentive audience to the vocal exertions of Mr and Mrs Allford who were professionally engaged, the summits of the South-West and other towers filled with lovers of the foreign weed and cheerful glass, the broad shadows of the mossy walls relieved by the scattered smiling groups employed in exploring the widely extended ruins adding to the general picturesque effect of the scene whilst the music of the band stationed in the Fountain Court reverberated through the 'proud baronial pile' devoted to ruin by the iron hand of Cromwell , these were amid the sources of enjoyment to the numerous visitors on whom the shades of evening stole with but too rapid strides to interrupt the pleasures of the day.

Friendly societies received a boost in membership following the passage of the 1832 Anatomy Act. This was enacted following the high-profile case of Burke and Hare in Edinburgh, which indicated the extent of the illegal trade in corpses. Prior to the legislation only the bodies of executed murderers could be dissected. This law permitted doctors and medical students access to corpses, often those of paupers that were unclaimed after death. It was not until 1844 that it became illegal for workhouse masters to sell corpses to medical schools. The 1832 legislation was very unpopular as there were widely held beliefs regarding the integrity of the corpse on Judgement Day. While Sheffield School of Anatomy was sacked by

Friendly Societies

an angry crowd in 1835, a more widespread response was to join or form a friendly society. These promised that a member, on death, would be buried rather than taken to the dissecting room. Ownership of the corpse and many commemorative rites were denied to paupers' next of kin. Some Poor Law Guardians replaced coffin nameplates with chalked numbers and forbade mourners from throwing soil on the coffin, entering the cemetery chapel or providing headstones. Stretford Burial Board stipulated that ownership of private graves reverted to the municipality if owners failed to install a headstone within six months of the first interment.

Registered friendly societies had to make returns every five years and their rules had to be confirmed by a barrister, John Tidd Pratt. He became the first Registrar of Friendly Societies and went on to draft the 1834 Poor Law Amendment Act. Since 1601 overseers had collected a poor rate from the richer people in a parish and distributed the money to the poor. This new legislation was designed to reduce how much was spent on the poor. Parishes were grouped into Unions. In each Union an elected Board of Guardians decided on the fate of the poor. Although the law was supposed to apply across the entire country it was never uniformly applied. In the north and west of England there were lower levels of entitlement than elsewhere. In many Unions the poorest people were expected to live in a workhouse. They were given a uniform and a poor diet and were expected to work. Families were split up and if they had any possessions they were supposed to give them up on going into the workhouse. The threat of this fate led people to join friendly societies. In the case of the Oddfellows, of the 30,074 lodges active in the 1870s nearly half (14,700) were established in the decade after 1835. By 1842 the Act had been applied to the whole of Lancashire, with the exception of Ashton-under-Lyne, Oldham and Rochdale. This was the county with the largest number of newly founded Oddfellow lodges between 1834 and 1841.

The spread of friendly societies was officially supported. In 1837 the Secretary of the Poor Law Commissioners Edwin Chadwick issued an 'Instructional letter addressed to various Boards of Guardians on their formation'. This stated that: 'The Commission trust that you will, each in his own neighbourhood, do all in your power to promote the formation of habits of forethought, of frugality, and self-dependence as will keep them [the able-bodied poor] from falling back into pauperism, by aiding the establishment of sick-clubs, savings banks and annuity societies.' On the other hand, some Dorset labourers who formed a friendly society were prosecuted because they had sworn an oath. They were convicted under the 1797 Unlawful Oaths Act and transported to Australia for seven years. One MP made the connection between allegations of insurrection and the Oddfellows. He admitted that he had been ignorant of the 1797 legislation and added: 'Indeed, if secret oaths were illegal and punishable by this Statute he was himself indictable as he belonged to the Society of Oddfellows and had taken a secret oath in that Society, over which presided at the time an eminent lawyer, now high in the administration of the law, who actually administered the oath to him'. The Oddfellows strove to show their loyalty. An oath of loyalty to the Society was replaced by a promise and in 1837 the Oddfellows declared that members were not permitted to sing or toast on religious or political topics and nor could strike pay be provided from its coffers. In 1841 it ruled that it would only make payments to members who were 'well attached to the Queen and Government'.

The 1834 legislation was in part based on the 1829 Friendly Societies Act which has been perceived as a significant stimulus to the growth of friendly societies. It was in turn a model for the 1875 Friendly Societies Act. Both friendly societies and Poor Law administrators were regulated in regions by district auditors and both sought to measure lives in similar ways. Friendly society membership did not prevent the elderly, the orphaned, the unemployed and the ill from spending time in the workhouse and Ancestry.co.uk has many records relating to individuals who were subject to this legislation.

CHARTISM

In 1832 the Great Reform Act extended the franchise to a few more men, but most adults were not permitted to vote. A movement, Chartism, arose to campaign for more people to be permitted to vote. The Chartists organised petitions calling for all men aged over 21 to be allowed to vote and for related social and political reforms. Chartism's peak of popularity was in the 1840s in the north of England. There working class people established their own newspaper and patrols of the streets in some towns. They were seen as a revolutionary threat. Special constables were sworn in and the army was mobilised to defend London against them. While it is worth checking the Chartist Ancestor site, your ancestors may have been effective trade-unionists but have shown little interest in overtly campaigning for wider political ambitions. Chartist Ancestor includes a databank of more than 10,500 known Chartists with information about addresses, occupations and involvement in various aspects of Chartism. There are biographies and notes on Chartist memorabilia and ephemera. See: http://www.chartistancestors.co.uk\.

Friendly societies provided places for people to learn how to organise, how to address a group and how to arrange meetings. They attracted respectable men who wanted a stake in society. Although the Oddfellow rule book, the 1841 *Laws for the Government of the Independent Order of Odd Fellows, of the Manchester Unity*, made it clear that fines could be imposed for 'singing an indecent or political song', and although many friendly societies had rules forbidding discussion of politics in the lodge, it is clear that there was considerable interest in Chartism. The Oddfellows split with most of the breakaway members from areas where Chartism was strongest. Oddfellow halls were used for Chartist meetings and the first issue of the *Odd Fellows Magazine* in 1839 had an editorial that supported the 'intrepid advocates of the just and meritorious "People's Charter"'. An attempt at a rising in 1839 involved men using Oddfellow ceremonial swords. In 1840 on Teesside two Oddfellow lodges agreed to invest £120 from lodge funds in shares in the Chartist Co-operative Society together with £75 of members' own money. Four months later this co-operative venture was registered under friendly society legislation. The Chartist Land Company was registered as a friendly society. In Dundee there was an Oddfellows Democratic Society which appointed men to deliver Chartist lectures across Fife. Abel Swann, a master tailor in Ashton-under-Lyne, was an active Oddfellow and chaired a Chartist lecture in Ashton under Lyne, in 1840. In 1841 the Chartist *Northern Star* cried 'hurrah! for the tailors and hurrah! for the Oddfellows' when an Oddfellow secretary and tailor agreed to stand for Parliament on a Chartist ticket. Six members of the Joseph Warburton Lodge of Oddfellows, in Middlesbrough, established in 1835, were Chartist activists. When one of the shareholders of the *Northern Star* was tried for seditious speeches, Newcastle Oddfellows contributed to his defence fund. Oddfellow funds supported radical printer Joshua Hobson, who produced both the *Northern Star* (between 1838 and 1844) and the radical *New Moral World* (between 1839 and 1841). William Aitken, a cotton spinner who later ran his own school and was imprisoned for sedition due to his Chartist activities, was central to the successful campaign to open an Oddfellows' Hall in Ashton in 1856. William Marcroft, 1822–94, was a Chartist and Oddfellow and William James Linton and Henry Hetherington, who were leading Chartists, edited the *Odd Fellows Magazine* during the period 1841–2. Abram Fielden of Todmorden was an active Chartist and Oddfellow. Following the death of Chartist Ben Rushton in 1853, a handloom weaver in Ovenden in the West Riding, 140 Oddfellows escorted his coffin and between 6,000 and 10,000 people are estimated to have attended his funeral. An account recorded that 'The coffin was carried by six veteran Chartists, and the splendid pall by six

Oddfellows'. The Chartists organised strikes and there were riots and other forms of protest, but still the franchise was not extended. Copies of the *Northern Star* (1837–52), are available at: http://www.ncse.ac.uk/index.html. Other Chartist newspapers are available through The National Archives.

There is a biographical account of the Chartist William Marcroft in the *Odd Fellows Magazine* of July 1857. The Affiliated Orders often published profiles of some of their prominent leaders. These biographies provide details of their backgrounds, roles at local, district and national level. There is often an illustration of the subject. The managing bodies also reported on their decisions through their publications. There are often names of members contained in these reports. These might be delegates to conferences or recipients of prizes. The Oddfellows have made over 190,000 Oddfellows documents available via its archive, https://www.Oddfellows.co.uk/join/?utm_source=facebook&utm_medium=social%20media&utm_campaign=membership&utm_term=archive. The material can be searched by a key word, period in time or document type. It includes magazines, minute books, reports and journals since the early nineteenth century, https://www.Oddfellows.co.uk/benefits/ historical-archive-content/. The *Odd Fellows Magazine*, 1829–1950, and the directories of the Manchester Unity Friendly Society, 1841–1941, are available on microfiche in a few libraries. They can also be purchased from Microform Imaging, Main Street, East Ardsley, Wakefield, West Yorkshire WF3 2AP, info@microform.co.uk, 019 2482 5700.

When looking for evidence of your ancestor's activities do not assume that those in friendly societies were only interested in Chartism. In addition to the association with Chartism, friendly societies maintained relationships with a range of political groups and provided opportunities for social advancement. Men could become lodge, then regional and then national executive members and could mix with wealthy men. In 1878 the AoF members included 17 peers, 4 bishops and 172 MPs. The Conservatives' Primrose

League had its own benefit society and some Tories ran their own local friendly societies. G.H. Roberts, elected in 1906 as one of the first Labour MPs, said that he 'graduated in the university of the friendly societies' and would not have been returned to the House 'but for the experience that he had gained in the friendly society movement'. The Liberals integrated 'Approved' friendly societies into their National Insurance Act, 1911.

A huge and wide range of items are associated with fraternal bodies, and during the nineteenth century in particular hundreds of artefacts were produced for members. There were medals (often called 'jewels') to be worn to demonstrate membership or rank or services rendered. There were collars and collarettes and sashes, aprons and gauntlets. Members wore ornamental chains of office and received certificates and marched with banners. Examples of certificates and posters often feature in society histories. One example is Walter G. Cooper, *The Ancient Order of Foresters Friendly Society, 150 years, 1834–1984* (1984). Some fraternal bodies obliged members to wear regalia, sometimes mourning regalia, to funerals. This could be ornate, the Oddfellows specified that 'death supporters' carry drawn swords to funeral processions. Members of the Markfield Female Friendly Society, which existed between 1823 and 1925, required members to attend the funerals of deceased members wearing 'a white ribbon and a pair of white gloves'. At a meeting of a Forester's Court there might be Beadles guarding proceedings. Their regalia included bugle horns (cow horns) and axes. The Senior and Junior Woodwards, who served summons, visited the sick and dispensed allowances and were in charge of Court property, each carried an axe. The regalia of the Nottingham Imperial Oddfellows included full-length medieval costumes. There were many opportunities for members to exhibit the regalia they acquired as there were a vast number of processions and parades in the late eighteenth century and throughout the nineteenth century. Some were to mark the opening of a prestigious building or a national event, such as a coronation. Others were in honour of the saint associated with a specific village or occurred on the same date, Whit Monday, for example, each year. They would be accompanied by church services, meals and sometimes the distribution of goods to the poor. Fraternal societies also paraded at the funeral of a member, marching from the church graveyard to pay the widow her dues. This reminded members and potential recruits of the benefits of membership.

A member of a friendly society may have had more than one certificate, which were issued on joining, if they advanced by gaining another degree or joined an additional lodge. Many members framed and displayed their certificates, an outward sign of their commitment. Lodges and Courts sometimes furnished their meeting places with ceremonial chairs for officers, wall boards listing the names of past officers and a gavel, mace or sceptre for the chair. Several of these exist in local museums and in lodges. In some cases, the items may not be on display but can be viewed on request. These items were full of symbols which indicate the ideas of the owners. Regalia was for members and some societies were only open to working men. Your ancestor may have owned items at home that showed his loyalty to a fraternal body. There were longcase clocks with Masonic and Odddfellow faces, trivets for flat-irons, spectacle cases, tie pins and lapel badges. There were also items that were presented to women on ladies' nights.

Many friendly societies and trade unions and Freemasons lodges ordered elaborate and expensive banners which were carried on church parades, to funerals and on a range of civic occasions, such as the opening of a local park or town hall. The People's History Museum, Manchester, has collated evidence of 216 friendly society banners, a small percentage of the thousands that contemporary sources indicate were made. One of the most popular images is of the Good Samaritan, as was noted in miners' leader Jack Lawson's recollection of the annual Durham miners' galas in the early twentieth century:

> First comes the great banner carried by picked men, who must know how to carry themselves, or their strength will avail them little . . . The colliery banner is almost a personality. Much thought has been given to colour, design and size. Deep debate on design and finance go to the making of it [. . .] No regimental flag is dearer to the soldier than the emblem, showing the Good Samaritan tending the stricken wayfarer, in a setting of red, blue and gold, is to the miner.

The Good Samaritan's appearance on banners might indicate that both unions and friendly societies had a continuing interest in the maintenance of a sense of reciprocity and mutual aid. The biblical parable is part of Jesus' response to being asked how eternal life might be attained. It concerns a travelling and relatively well-resourced outsider, the Samaritan, who helps a robbed and injured man who has been ignored by the representatives of established aid agencies. At some risk to himself, the Samaritan gives him alcohol and makes a payment towards his healthcare. He promotes a cycle of exchange when he asks another man, an innkeeper, to provide for the injured man and be repaid later. There is surveillance of the sick as he promises to return and check on the effects of the care.

Seeing the image on a banner might well have brought to mind hospitals' admission policies. These were determined not by doctors, but by hospital patrons. For much of the nineteenth century for a poor person to be treated in many hospitals required them to present a letter from a subscriber or governor. Prospective patients needed a subscriber who was prepared to recommend them, just as the Good Samaritan vouched for the injured traveller to the innkeeper who was to care for him. Friendly societies increasingly donated to hospitals and expected members to receive medical treatment. The opening ceremony of Huddersfield Infirmary was attended by the Manchester Unity Odd Fellows, Royal Foresters, Ancient Order of Shepherds and various local societies. By the 1870s the annual Friendly Societies Demonstration made several hundred pounds each year for the hospital. There are numerous records of such activities. The Oddfellows donated to hospitals in, for example, Northampton, Wakefield and Huddersfield and secured places for their members. Societies also sent a Sick Visitor to ill members to make payments and to ensure compliance with the rules relating to illness. Your ancestor might well have either been a Visitor or been visited. In 1892 a Foresters' Chief Ranger (Court chairman) in Loughborough was fined £1 and had to resign from his post after he was seen to be drunk while also claiming from the Sick Fund. In the 1930s Albert Fox was a Sick Visitor in the Loyal Adventurers of the Peak, an Oddfellows lodge in Taddington, Derbyshire. He recalled that one Visitor caught a sick member pruning his roses and had the sick pay stopped. The most common medical item discussed in the minutes of local meetings was suspicions about the merits of claims. In the parable the Samaritan was granted life. He ascended the hierarchy of society, from outsider to immortal. A member of a friendly society could rise through the ranks and gain, if not power over life and death, then at least power and status. Furthermore, there was provision for the name of a departed brother to be if not immortalised, then at least commemorated.

The details of one Grand Procession were recorded on a poster which was sold for a penny; there is a copy of it in Sheffield Masonic Hall, Tapton Hall, Sheffield. The procession of 4 October 1797 went from St Paul's Church to the General Infirmary in Sheffield. It had three sections. There were a dozen lodges of Freemasons. After the Craft Masons came the Royal Arch Companions and then came Knight Companion Witham bearing the Knight Templars' Banner and after him came the Knight Templar Companions. In the second section were people associated with the church and the hospital, the Clerk of Works, Secretary and Architect, medics, clerics and magistrates. Friendly societies were in the third section. The dates of their foundations are given from the Tailor's Society, 1720, to the Loyal Independent Volunteer Sick Club, 1794. It is clear that others, not listed, joined the procession. There was a dinner afterwards at the Angel Inn. The poster was later reprinted in the *Independent*, 13 May 1854, from a leaflet published by James Montgomery and is available at: https://www.sheffieldhistory.co.uk/forums/topic/12381-procession-on-the-opening-of-the-infirmary-1797/?tab=comments#comment-102689.

As well as grouping together in Affiliated Orders, friendly societies could flourish if they gained the financial support of wealthier people. Some societies had close contact with doctors or solicitors and others had patrons. These men might well be made Honorary members and wear a variation of the members' regalia. County societies were often well-funded being run and often partially subsidised by the local gentry. They existed in the south of England, wholly or partially in twenty counties. Members had no voting rights. The Hampshire Friendly Society served the population of that county between 1824 and 1989. Honorary members paid at least £10, or an annual subscription of at least £1 and were not permitted to draw any emoluments from the Society. Its principal purpose was to provide assurances against sickness and death, with a range of subscription rates and commensurate benefits to suit different income levels. Perhaps because it was not a mutual aid society the Hampshire Friendly Society could not rely on a fraternal ethos. Its patrons created a systematic set of administrative procedures to prevent abuse. This has resulted in the creation of some rich records of the health of individuals. When the Society was first set up, members were able to subscribe for sickness benefits; pensions; death benefits; and childhood endowments, which yielded a given sum of money when children reached their 14th or 21st birthdays. Although an increasing proportion of new members appear to have registered for pensions or death benefits only, by 1914 the Society still had more than 7,500 members who qualified for some form of sickness pay, and more than 10,000 assured members overall. It operated a deposit scheme from 1867 and in 1900, when the Society had 8,998 assured members, its total membership (including deposit members) was 14,876. There have been several academic studies of the records of over 5,500 men who joined between 1824 and 1939. Records are held at Hampshire Record Office Sussex Street, Winchester, Hampshire.

Lodge and Court records can reveal who was elected to which posts, attendance, payments made, deaths and sickness. Courts also held proposition books indicating the names, addresses, ages and marital status of those joining the AoF and their proposer and seconder. There are also some membership and sickness registers and data about funerals. From the contributions data of Court Unity, 5340, which met at the Star Inn, Burnham, Essex it can be seen that George Harris paid the Court Secretary, Thomas Ambrose, an entry fee on 18 February 1874. This was 15*s*. He then started to pay monthly contributions of 2*s*. 3*d*. As this was based on his age, it suggests that he was 29 when he joined. He was entitled to sick pay of 14*s*. for twenty-six weeks, 7*s*. for a further twenty-six weeks and 5*s*. after that. He paid 1*s*. 6*d*. to the Doctor's Fund in order to receive medicines and attendance when ill but he did not subscribe to the Widows and Orphans Fund. From these sorts of records it is clear that friendly society membership was not for everybody. In the 1880s an 18-year-old in the AoF could pay in 1*s*. per annum and expect to receive 1*s*. per week, if ill. Insuring for 20*s*. per week would cost 20*s*. and 3*d*. per annum. The cost rose with age and for a 39-year-old it was 1*s*. 6*d*. and 30*s*. 4*d*. respectively. Funeral benefits insurance for a £1 funeral also rose in price from 3*d*. and a farthing for an 18-year-old to 10*d*. for a 50-year-old. There were different rates depending if a member lived in a rural area or an urban one. In the 1870s the average weekly wage for a Cornish miner was 18*s*. a week. To receive 12*s*. a week for the first six months off work and 9*s*. for the next six months and a death benefit of £12 for himself and £8 for his wife, a 30-year-old married man in a Cornish town who was a Forester would need to pay 21*s*. 6*d*. a year. This figure had risen to about 30*s*. by 1900. The Oddfellows charged a little more (the same man might pay 27*s*. per annum). It recruited to the age of 45, while the Foresters only admitted those aged 35 or younger. The impact was that many who joined soon left, in effect subsidising those who remained.

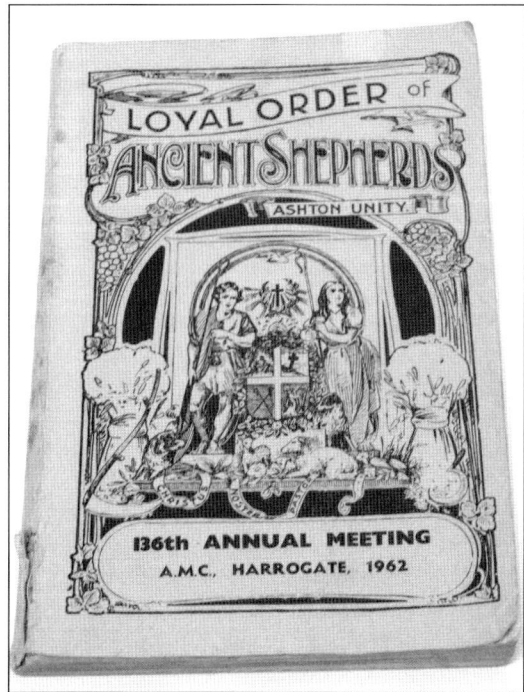

This booklet from the Annual Movable Conference (AMC) of the Loyal Order of Ancient Shepherds, Ashton Unity has many names and details inside. There are records of the Society in Dundee City Archives, West Yorkshire Archives Service, Calderdale and in private collections. (Author's collection)

Societies for women tended to be in those areas where women earned money, for example, in the mills of Lancashire or as straw plaiters in Bedfordshire. Even then many of these societies were subsidised by wealthy patrons. Male agricultural labourers earned about 10s. a week. Few could not afford the weekly payments societies demanded. They might pay into a village society which charged less, or only put money aside for their funeral, not their sickness. One disadvantage of village societies was they were not always actuarially sound. While members might well have felt that they could trust others in their group not to make false claims on funds and to treat them well, if there was a localised difficulty, fatalities following a fishing accident, the mine running low on coal to dig or a poor harvest, then the risk of the society folding was high. As most societies were open only to men who had not reached the age of 40, a man who had paid into a club all his working life might be left impoverished just at the time that he needed the money.

The larger friendly societies had the funds to be charitable, but payments to members were regulated. Nevertheless, friendly societies, also made charitable donations, and in this sense they were similar to Freemasons. In 1800 in Manchester a union of friendly societies collected donations, purchased in bulk, distributed food cheaply to the poor and was reputed to have saved its members £5,000. Numerous lifeboats were donated by friendly societies and Freemasons. Moreover, both types of organisations raised money for charity and made payments to members who had met with misfortune. Members could appeal to their lodges for help beyond that which was expected, and then their region and finally the national organisers. For example, at its annual delegate meetings the Foresters decided on which members were worthy of additional, charitable, help from its funds. You can find details of the incomes of people whose sickness payments had concluded but, who still unable to work, had made an appeal to the charitable funds of the Order. Between lodges (or Courts) and national decision-making lay the Districts. There were 218 AoF Districts in 1880 in England, Scotland had 20 by 1884 and Wales reached 26 by 1894. Some of the reports, information about officials and decisions still exist and can be mined for data about individuals, including their places of residence, roles within the AoF and attendance records. Brother John Fisher of Court Star of Surrey, No. 1392, first attended a meeting in July 1851 and made his final recorded appearance at one in July 1899. He was a long-time Court Secretary, but also held posts at District level. One of the tasks of Districts was to administer payments for members' widows' funerals. There were account funds and in some cases there remain lists of members and their widows with ages and dates of death. A Widows and Orphans Fund often also existed and details of recipients and the ages of children were sometimes recorded. Records exist, but there are many gaps and you may not find details for your ancestor.

Newspapers (see Chapter 3) are a useful source for information about charitable activity such as when the Druids (a friendly society) held a concert at which the opportunity was taken to present an injured brother a sum of £40 and on another occasion £25 was given to a disabled member. A local newspaper reported that the Crewe Co-operative Industrial and Friendly Society ran a dentist and sick benefit club for employees, donated to local people, famine relief in India, locked-out engineers in 1897 and the local hospital, to which it also recommended patients. Other friendly societies were run by churches, businesses and nationalist groups. The Salvation Army and numerous Sunday schools ran their own friendly societies. There was a considerable overlap between charities and fraternal aid.

> **Personal Accounts of Charity**
> Autobiographies can also be a useful source for details of friendly society charity. After a clergyman who controlled a local charity refused help to silkweaver Joseph Gutteridge, an atheist, his neighbours saved his wife and five children from the workhouse or starvation, and the Oddfellows helped him to bury his fourth child, who died from smallpox. In the autobiography he published when he was aged 77 Gutteridge described how on one occasion his father was taken ill: 'During a violent fit of coughing he ruptured a blood vessel. As soon as he possibly could he insisted on going back to work again, being in a manner compelled to take this step by the fact that the Benefit Society to which he belonged had for some time suspended payment for sickness.' Gutteridge himself received 10s. a week from the Oddfellows during illness in 1851 and was the beneficiary of Oddfellow charity. In 1845 he reported that:
>
> > We had been without work for many weeks, but I had made up my mind that come what might I would not appeal to the parish for relief. Help at last came from an unexpected quarter. On New Year's Day 1845 while acting as a door keeper at a

Friendly Societies

> ball given by the Philanthropic Lodge of the Manchester Unity of Odd Fellows at St Mary's Hall, my despondency attracted the attention of two senior officers of the lodge, Thomas Barnes and James Rushton. I had cause to be down hearted; my boy lay at home dead and I had not the means to bury him. The two gentlemen enquired the cause of my grief and on learning my story they expressed their sympathy and when the ball broke up at about two o'clock in the morning they bade me stay awhile and presented me with a sum of money obtained from friends which enabled me to bury my child decently.

In 1837 a quarter of the deaths in Glasgow were due to typhus, a disease closely associated with poverty. When James Burn's family caught typhus he was the recipient of considerable Oddfellow generosity:

> As soon as my calamity became known to the Odd Fellows' Lodges several of them sent me various sums of money. The 'Banks of Clyde' in Greenock, of which I was a member cleared me off their books and sent me three pounds and ten shillings. I may remark that I had long been out of benefit in consequence of not being able to pay my contribution. One of the lodges in Edinburgh sent two pounds. One of the country lodges also sent the same sum; and two of the town lodges sent five pounds between them.

Although measurement of the membership of friendly societies has long been difficult, even after registration was encouraged, a reasonable estimate is that the number of members grew from about 600,000 in 1793. In 1872 the Royal Commission on Friendly Societies estimated that total friendly society membership was over 4 million and that of the 2 million registered friendly society members in England and Wales only 43,417 were in societies controlled by honorary members. The Royal Commission on Friendly Societies 1874 reported that there were 460 female-registered friendly societies in England and Wales with a total membership of 27,107. This membership did not include members of 177 other societies that made no return, nor the many unregistered societies. Other estimates put the overall figure at 6 million members. Trade-union membership was about 1 million. In 1898 the Chief Registrar of Friendly Societies put membership at just over 8 million. In 1900 the AoF and the Oddfellows alone had about 2 million members. They both collected and distributed significant sums of money. Between 1900 and 1911 the AoF paid out an average of over £600,000 a year in sickness payments and £135,000 in death benefits. Estimates for numbers in 1910 vary between 6.3 million and maybe 9.5 million friendly society members.

1911: NATIONAL INSURANCE

In 1911 legislation to provide National Insurance for most working people was passed. Between 1912 and 1948 this system of compulsory health insurance for the lower paid employed was administered by 'Approved Societies' which included friendly societies, trade unions and commercial insurance companies. The scheme involved a modest state subsidy and was built upon the payment traditions and structures of the friendly societies and trade unions, some of which already offered unemployment pay. All employed persons aged between 16 and 70, if they earned less than £160 per annum or were manual labourers in the same age group regardless of earnings, had to join a society which had been approved by the government. The legislation provided between 11 and 12.4 million people with health insurance in 1912 and this figure rose in subsequent years as the population grew and the threshold for eligibility changed (in 1920 the amount earned for coverage was raised to £250, while in 1928 the upper age was reduced to 65, and finally in 1937 those younger than 16 were also covered if employed). By 1942 some 21 million workers were covered. If they lost their jobs they did not contribute to the scheme but were still allowed to claim. Employers paid 3*d*., male workers 4*d*., women 3*d*. and the government 2*d*. a week. Women workers whose husbands were also insured qualified for double benefit.

Contributions were paid through a lengthy process. Employers purchased stamps at the post office, fixed them to the workers' contribution cards and deducted the workers' portion directly from wages. These cards were returned to the member's Approved Society, which returned them to the Ministry as proof of contributory income. Although the day-to-day administrative decisions were supposedly left to the Approved Societies, in practice transactions between centre and each society were monitored through the process of audit. Collectively, the Controller, the official auditors and Government Actuary determined the ways in which the scheme developed. The process of audit was expensive and reduced the local autonomy of mutuals' branches. Every one of these had to keep track of nine different account books, twenty-one different categories of insured people and twenty-two different items of information about each member. Changes were made to the scheme in almost every year between 1913 and 1945. The Oddfellows lamented that 'We never dreamed . . . we would be so governed by regulations. We had no idea that the Treasury grant would be bound up in so much red tape'. You may find insurance stamps among your ancestor's possessions as much of the administration was done by unpaid friendly society officers.

Although through the legislation some friendly societies and trade unions were yoked together, the Act also opened up divisions between and within fraternal bodies. From the 1890s, and in some cases earlier, the major friendly societies admitted women. There was a considerable influx of women following the 1911 Act. As a result, far fewer friendly society meetings were held in pubs. This shift separated the friendly societies from the Freemasons' lodges where men continued to meet and drink together. During a period dominated by the interwar depression, material considerations came to dominate and democratic practices withered away. Some members felt that traditions of fellowship and sociability were marginalised. The shift in focus was in part because the tasks required of Approved Societies by the government were complicated. The friendly societies had to create and support unplanned new branches of their businesses as well as maintain their old ones. Friendly societies and trade unions, designed for mutual aid, found it difficult to adapt to their new roles as officially 'Approved Societies'. They were obliged to focus on cash benefits rather than their moral and educational roles. The workload of local secretaries increased as non-Approved Societies closed or merged with approved ones. In the Exeter area the Oddfellows opened 4 female lodges and recruited 2,500 members. The voluntary and part-time Provincial Corresponding Secretary resigned and was replaced by a full-timer on a salary of £150 a year. Any money that the friendly societies made was held by the government. The actuarial conservatism of the system benefitted Treasury coffers at the expense of the mutual sector. The conservatism of the actuarial science practised by the Exchequer was such that by 1938 over £220 million of society investments were in centralised reserve funds. This was more than the assets of the Unemployment Fund (£130 million) and the Pensions Fund (£50 million) combined. The societies had lost much of their independence.

> **RITUALS REMEMBERED**
> Despite the focus on insurance, an interest in social and ritual was retained. Ritual was practised in order to comply with the rules, to demonstrate respect and affiliation, to satisfy emotional requirements and nourish relationships, to strengthen social bonds and for pleasure. It had practical applications, being useful for checking on members' status, informing them of the ideals of the fraternity, structuring change and networks within the organisation and uniting members across time and space in common activities. Bill Needham, 1904–83, joined the Manchester

Unity Oddfellows in 1919. His recollections, recorded in the 1980s, suggest the importance of the pub, the continuing significance of secrecy and the mixture of formal regulations and boisterousness. His testimony provides insights into how members understand their own past and that of their fraternal association and how respectable civility and rougher conviviality were often merged. Secrecy and rituals were integral to the ethos of many fraternal organisations.

> We had a monthly meeting and it was always held in a pub ... It was run properly then, with a full committee, secretary, the lot ... We always had a club room ... There used to be a member on the door and he were called the Tyler and nobody strange would get into that meeting because you had a secret sort of code. You would have to knock on the door with your first two knuckles, twice. The Tyler would be behind the door, fastened on the inside. He would open the door and say 'Brother Needham wishes to be admitted'.

Needham went on to recount how an initiate would be blindfolded and have a hot poker placed very near his bottom. He added 'We had quite a lot of laughs about that. It was alright for us as knew, but it was them that didn't know, you see'. Personal accounts of the 1930s indicate both why your ancestor might have been an enthusiastic member of a friendly society and how an ancestor may have seen the society as little more than an administrative body.

Other problems arose because of the 1911 Act. The relationship between doctors and friendly societies, which had been strained prior to 1911, worsened in part due to the structures created to connect the administrative and professional and clinical bodies involved in administering the National Insurance scheme. Prior to the legislation many doctors were employed by friendly societies and there was friction regarding clinical judgments, professional status and pay. Following the legislation doctors were paid per Approved Society patient on their panel and this encouraged GPs to recruit the maximum number of panel patients and to spend the minimum time treating them. Friendly societies tended to see doctors as part of the problem. When the total amount of sickness benefits paid to claimants rose in 1927, partly due to an influenza epidemic, the Foresters claimed that this was also due to 'loose certification for sickness payments by panel doctors'.

The legislation had the effect of associating friendly societies with party politics. They tended to oppose a state-run national health service as that would take power away from them. In 1929 a Past Grand Master of the Oddfellows and its Parliamentary Agent produced a pamphlet which was sent to every lodge secretary. It was headed, 'National Health Insurance, created by Liberals, raided by Tories, threatened by Socialists' and it was published by the Liberal Publication Department. Stanley Baldwin, a Forester and an Oddfellow, was prime minister for over seven years between 1923 and 1937, including during the 1926 General Strike. He was associated with appeasement and was perceived as the de facto prime minister in a coalition government headed by Ramsay MacDonald, the Labour prime minister who was expelled from the Labour Party. Neville Chamberlain, who succeeded Baldwin as PM, was a member of the Ancient Order of Foresters. This association with Conservatives and Liberals may not have bolstered the societies' claim to be politically neutral. Between 1915 and 1931 the Secretary of an Approved Society, the commercial Prudential, was Sir George May. He also headed the Committee on National Expenditure. In 1931 its report proposed major cuts to welfare provision. The Labour Cabinet split over implementation of the report and the government fell from power. By 1945 the Labour Party had run innovative health services at local level, had categorised all the Approved Societies as inappropriate bodies to run national insurances and had decided that it favoured a comprehensive health plan run at national, not municipal or local, level by state officials. Labour was largely funded by and supportive of the trade unions but it was also part of the wartime coalition government which abolished 'approved' status with the establishment of a Ministry of National Insurance in 1944 and it was in government when the National Insurance Act was passed in 1946. However they voted, your ancestor's activity within a friendly society may have meant that it was assumed that he or she was not a Labour supporter.

Friendly societies became associated with the strict enforcement of rules. In Taddington, Derbyshire Oddfellow Frank Bagshaw recalled that in the 1930s, 'If you were off work they used to have a Sick Visitor, and he'd just drop in on you, any time. If he saw you cleaning your boots, you were in trouble'. In nearby Disley Margaret Graham recalled that, 'If you were on the club you couldn't go out after 7 o'clock at night otherwise you lost your club money'. Monitoring the ill on behalf of the government, enforcing its labyrinthine regulations and blaming medical professionals when problems arose did little to improve the public image of the societies. Whereas in the past collecting contributions, processing claims and policing against fraud had been balanced by the pleasures of voluntary thrift, proud parades and democratic self-government, the 1911 Act shifted the focus. The 'sympathetic visitor' who brought 'into the house of the afflicted brother . . . not only the benefit which the sick member has contributed for, but also a word of cheer and comfort from his brothers in the Order' was replaced, said the *Odd Fellows Magazine* in 1913, by 'cold officialism that will only perform so much service for so much monetary consideration'. Following the legislation the formerly 'warm-hearted, sympathetic sick visitor [now] rushes round on Friday night or Saturday, hands the money in . . . takes a receipt for the benefit and goes'. The effect of being 'approved' was, as one Oddfellow pointed out in the *Odd Fellows Magazine*, in June 1915, that members became 'actuarial friendly society men rather than actual friendly society men [whose] souls were in pawn to the devil of arithmetic, who blew our ideals sky-high'.

Friendly societies continued to provide support for the ill. The Alderston Convalescent Home was established in 1925 by the Scottish Rural Workers Friendly Society for the benefit of rural workers. This benefit encouraged and sustained membership. It was one of three relatively Scottish convalescent homes established by friendly societies between 1900 and 1939. The other two were Ashgrove House, near Dunoon, opened in 1903 by the Rechabites, and Orwell House, established in 1909 at Kinbuck, near Dunblane by the Scottish Foresters' Convalescent Home Benevolent Society. Many societies subscribed to the larger independent homes such as the Dunoon Homes, Kilmun, the Mission Coast Home and the Glasgow Convalescent Home. The number of patients recommended for admission to a convalescent home depended on the amount subscribed. The National Amalgamated Approved Society subscribed £186 per year and was entitled to recommend 186 members to the Dunoon Homes. The Grand Order of Israel Friendly Society, with an annual subscription of £1 was only entitled to recommend one patient annually. Trade unions and the Freemasons also ran their own convalescence homes. Although many of the homes have closed, when you next take a trip to the seaside you might well spot one of the buildings where an ancestor stayed while recovering from an illness.

FURTHER ROLES FOR THE STATE

The creation of the NHS after the Second World War and the involvement of Whitehall, rather than Approved Societies, in the running national insurance, led to a decline in friendly societies. In 1945 8.7 million people were members of friendly societies. If widows, members of female societies, honorary members (of whom there were 1,913) and other members are included, there were over a million members of the Oddfellows, which also had over a million National Health Insurance 'state members'. In that year, there was a decrease in Oddfellow membership of 6,800 members. People could go to the state, rather than the mutual sector, for support during periods of ill health. In 1945 an Oddfellows Special Conference decided that 'every lodge should be built like the nation, upon the basis of the family and be encouraged to have men women and juvenile members. There was also a call for 'the reorganisation of the fellowship side of the Society' in order to mimic 'the idea of Masonry, where the Ritual and Social side takes precedence over the charitable or Insurance side'. The Oddfellows Grand Master called for a revival of social activities, for more lodges to open and said that it was 'necessary to encourage the family membership of a lodge – father, mother and children – so that in future new lodges must make provision to that effect and admit females and junior members'. Woolwich formed the first family lodge and there was an increased interest in ensuring that women could contribute to the Oddfellows in a variety of ways, including being elected to attend the annual conference.

Despite the efforts of some activists, there was no revival. A further 9,500 left the Oddfellows in 1946 and almost twice as many as that in 1947 (18,600). The decrease doubled again to 35,500 in 1948. This was largely due to lapses rather than deaths. Men returned from the services and did not resume payment. It was difficult to trace many of them and as the level of contributions also rose, some other members left. In 1948 two years after the National Insurance Act, 205 of its lodges had closed and, including 2,400 juveniles, there were only 6,170 new joiners. This was the lowest figure for the Oddfellows in over fifty years. While this rapid decline was not entirely due to the legislation, it appears that so unpopular had the Approved Societies become that as soon as the opportunity to leave arose then reliance on the state became widespread. Mutuals had become associated with a system in which seven different government departments were involved, with three different and mutually exclusive benefits for unemployment, three different types of pension and different schemes for the blind, the disabled, those with industrial injuries and the sick who earned less than £250 a year. Mutuality rested upon local, democratic, supportive lodges in which the government was not interested. It imposed a system on the mutuals which was efficient only in its terms. Having shifted their perspectives, the mutuals were then relieved of their administrative role and had to struggle to find a new one.

William Beveridge's 1942 report *Social Insurance and Allied Services* was the basis for many of the changes within welfare provision made by the government in the late 1940s. Supported by the National Deposit Friendly Society, he was also responsible for *Voluntary Action* (1948) and a supplementary volume, *The Evidence for Voluntary Action* (1949). Both contain much about friendly societies, including personal testimony and the results of a survey of 150 members of friendly societies. Comments are anonymous so you can only tell that it was said by people classified by age and social status, such as 'working-class housewife, 55' or 'middle-class man, 45'. However, you can get a clear sense of how members saw the changes brought about through the introduction of state provision for health and funerals.

The Oddfellows had over a million members in 1860 and maybe 2 million between the wars when people had to join an Approved Society if they were to be able to contribute towards, and claim from, National Insurance. Some districts admitted no juniors in 1953 and the overall number fell from 52,667 in 1951 to 50,648, while 20,000 adults also left the Oddfellows. In 1955 half of the 3,000 lodges did not accept a single new member. The number of branches of the larger Affiliated Oders, the Oddfellows, the Rechabites, the Foresters, Shepherds, Free Gardeners and Sons of Temperance, fell from around 16,000 in 1945 to 11,000 in 1955 (3,000 of these being Oddfellow lodges) and adult membership from 2,150,000 to 1,350,000 (about 500,000 of them being Oddfellows) during the same period. Some 61,216 had left these societies during the previous year. Between 1964 and 1986 the Oddfellows started to produce a magazine for junior members, the *Mini Link*. Some 7,000 birthday cards were dispatched to junior members by Joan Henry ('Aunty Jo'). You might come across one or copies of the magazine. There were other publications. The monthly *Odd Fellows Magazine* contains the names of numerous active members and their achievements and when there were family connections these were often mentioned. Pat Morgan joined the Oddfellows aged 16 in 1956 and rose to become chair. On one occasion she held a lodge dinner at which the guests of honour were the Grand Master, her father, and the Provincial Grand Master, her mother. Often families would take their holidays at the seaside where a parent would attend the conference and the children would play on the beach. Reports of these gatherings appeared not just in the Oddfellows press but the local seaside newspapers as well. There are also numerous types of ephemera left over from these efforts to attract young people and to organise social events. In Daniel Weinbren's *The Oddfellows* (2012) there are images of a ticket for a Field Day, a photo of a play produced by junior Oddfellows and a party arranged by members of the Edmondscote and Stratford-upon-Avon district Intermediate Lodge, 1964. A check through the personal collection of an ancestor who was active in a friendly society is likely to yield other examples of material which will enable you to gain a sense of the activities of the time and the place where your ancestor was active in a friendly society. It can be helpful to talk about photographs or memorabilia to anybody who might recall the items being used. This may well prompt further information and you might learn more about your ancestor's involvement.

It was only after the passage of the Trustee Investment Act 1961 that friendly societies had the power to invest in equity investments and other restrictions were only lifted following further Acts. Legislation categorised the societies with insurance companies and constraints on the decisions which could be made at branch level were introduced. In effect, branch autonomy was reduced. During the half century after the war, branches closed and members, unwilling to travel further to meetings left. This led to further closures. In 1966 an Oddfellow Past Grand Master argued for the society to return 'to the simple things in Odd Fellowship which were exactly the same as they were 150 years ago. We are drifting into commercialism. . . Odd Fellowship is not something to sell – it is something to give for the benefit of the human race . . . fraternity was of greater importance than finance'. Still the number of Oddfellow lodges fell. There were 2,453 registered lodges in 1972, 1,565 a decade later and 171 by 1992. As people moved to the suburbs away from the societies' properties, the halls became little-used and sold. Many of the buildings can still be found. The University of Manchester's Language Centre is in a former Oddfellows Hall. The problems that arose when lodges closed were recognised. However, keeping them open was difficult. For example, in the 1920s the forty lodges of the Worcester area opened their own District Hall with a bar and a dance hall which was the base for a dance school. However, numbers dwindled and the hall was sold in 2000.

In the 1990s leading building societies became shareholder-owned banks, some leading mutual insurers demutualised, co-operative retailers' share of the market declined and trade-union membership fell away. Many of the Affiliated Orders closed. There were sixty-six in 1945 and only twenty in 1990. The Independent Order of Rechabites, at one time one of the largest of the UK's friendly societies, took the decision to close its branches ('tents'), cease to have meetings for members, to centralise its financial operations and to rebrand as Healthy Investment. Oddfellow membership was below 100,000.

The story of the Oddfellows' Old Elm Lodge, Chipping Norton can be used to stand for the fate of many lodges. In 1924 it had over 900 'state members' and 819 voluntary members who wished to supplement their National Insurance benefits. Voluntary membership fell to 765 by 1930 and 707 by 1940, while the average age grew from 35 in 1906 to 43 in 1931. In 1947 the district chair appealed to members to 'double their efforts to maintain the voluntary side of the Order'. The Old Elm did not fare as badly as other lodges in that it still had 587 members in 1950, but only 383 a decade later. In 1970 there were 340 and 214 by 1982, a year when only one person joined the lodge. Posts were unfilled and there were few young people. By the mid-1980s 40 per cent of the members were aged 65 or over, and the Society launched a booklet about bereavement, *Dealing with death*. The business affairs were transferred to a financial lodge in Cheltenham and although the lodge continued to exist for a little longer, its meetings ceased to occur. This story has echoes across the field of friendly societies. If your ancestor's friendly society branch disappeared in the twentieth century, then it may well have shared a similar fate to the Old Elm.

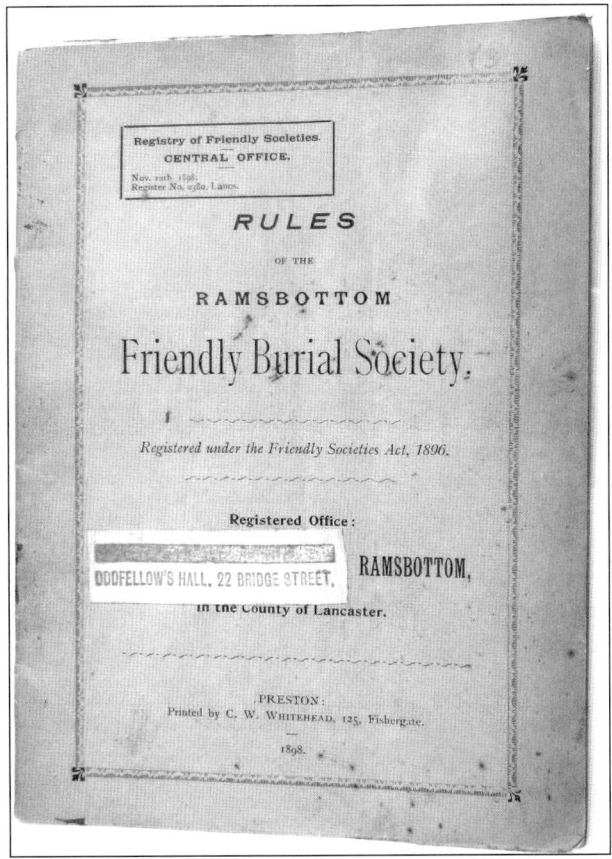

Many friendly societies, and many unions, found it hard to survive if hit by the need for a large amount of expenditure over a short period of time. Reasons for this might be disease, widespread redundancies or a cohort of founding members becoming pensioners at around the same time when there were insufficient younger members to support them. One alternative to closure was amalgamation with a larger body. In this case the Ramsbottom Friendly Burial Society became part of the Oddfellows. (Author's collection)

Chapter 7

TRADE UNIONS

If you have established that your ancestor was in a trade union, then, before looking for specific evidence of your ancestor's activities, you may wish to take an overview of the historical framework. You will then be able to make sense of developments over time and know which specialist archives are likely to be of value to you. In this chapter there is a definition of trade unions and an outline of developments since the late eighteenth century. There is also consideration of the importance of rituals, film as a source and how unions have been central to communities.

There has long been an overlap between different fraternal organisations and they have often shared functions. There have been many definitions. The left-wing intellectuals Beatrice and Sidney Webb called a union 'a continuous association of wage-earners for the purpose of maintaining or improving the conditions of their working lives'. This insistence on continuity was not one adopted in the Trade Union Act of 1871. In this it was suggested that the term 'trade union' meant 'such combination, whether temporary or permanent, for regulating the relations between workmen and masters, or between workmen and workmen, or between masters and masters, or for imposing restrictive conditions on the conduct of any trade or business'. As a generality, unions arose when employees joined together to present a collective front in negotiations with an employer and to provide a measure of security for its members. They were designed to protect and promote common interests, negotiate, sometimes through collective bargaining, wages and working conditions, regulate relations between members and also between members and their employer, make new demands and help to settle grievances. Using a definition of unions as popularly understood, the Trade Union Ancestors site includes a complete listing of all British trade unions known to have existed over the past 200 years, http://www.unionancestors.co.uk. For a published perspective there is helpful guidance in Mark Crail's *Tracing Your Labour Movement Ancestors: A Guide for Family Historians* (2009).

SINCE THE 1790s
In the 1790s there was concern among employers and the wealthy that workers, angry at rising food prices, were being radicalised. Strikes, it was argued by many in positions of authority, could adversely affect the course of the war that was being fought against the revolutionary French, led by Napoleon. As noted in Chapter 6, legislation attempted to place friendly societies, which helped working people to pay for their own healthcare and reduced the rates, and Freemasons on one side of the law and trade unions on the other. The government sought to support those organisations of which it approved and to outlaw the rest. However, that distinction was difficult to maintain as there was a continuum between the different fraternal bodies. In 1799 George Rose, the Secretary to the Treasury and the person responsible for the 1793 Friendly Societies Act, introduced the bill that was to become the Combination Act of 1799. This took the legislation that already outlawed combinations among the wool hatters (1749), clothiers (1775), silk weavers (1777), paper makers (1795) and millwrights (1799) and generalised it, making it illegal for workers to join together in order to call for shorter hours or more pay. There was both continuity with prior legislation and a significant policy development. The Act of 1800 slightly moderated the 1799 Act but trade unions were effectively made illegal. In the absence of this vehicle for the expression of collective demands, when in 1811–13 wages fell weavers started to

break machinery in protest. Others formed illegal unions and thousands of people were convicted. The legislation was not repealed at the conclusion of the war, in 1815, but remained in place until 1824.

In 1824 the Combination Acts were repealed and trade unions excluded from prosecution. This change in the law was largely the responsibility of a radical worker and strike leader who had established his own business in 1800 – Francis Place. Records of Francis Place can be found at the British Museum. For material about his radical contemporaries see: http://www.british-history.ac.uk. Following the repeal there was a vast number of strikes, many of them high-profile. In 1825 fresh legislation revoked much of the legislation of 1824. Unions were prohibited from collectively bargaining in order to try to improve pay or conditions and the right to strike was supressed. The rights to combination and collective bargaining were retained and bargaining on wages and hours were maintained. Unions were regarded as suspicious by the authorities and those who joined continued to use secret passwords and initiation rites. Trade societies were subject to the common law of conspiracy and there were many prosecutions. Negotiations about apprenticeships, hours, wages and conditions continued and trade societies continued to maintain their friendly society functions of making payments for sickness and death.

In 1834 six men in Tolpuddle, Dorset, formed a society in which initiates were led into a room, were shown a picture of a skeleton and swore an oath. Convicted under the 1797 Unlawful Oaths Act, they were transported to Australia. The verdict was toasted by officers of the Masonic UGLE who urged Masonic lodges to check that their exemptions were in order. However, the cause of the Tolpuddle Martyrs was taken up by the wider trade-union movement. After protests, the labourers were released in 1836 and 1837. The Trades Union Congress (TUC) holds an annual festival to celebrate the Martyrs in Dorset and there is a museum in the village: http://tolpuddlemartyrs.org.uk/museum. In 1838, perhaps because conspirators were needed to justify the continuation of legislation to prevent trade unions, at the trial of five cotton spinners for conspiracy and murder, trade unions were once again represented as dangerous secret societies.

Although trade-union records were often secret, some documents of this period survive. The *Trades Newspaper and Mechanics Weekly Journal*, 1825–8 is held in the Working Class Movement Library: https://www.wcml.org.uk. The Bishopsgate Institute, 230 Bishopsgate, London, EC2M 4QH also holds some relevant records, trade-union books and pamphlets and personal papers. See: http://www.bishopsgate.org.uk/content.aspx?CategoryID =1519. These include the papers of trade-unionist and local MP George Howell, 1833–1910. He was active in the Operative Bricklayers' Society and later served as Secretary of the London Trades Council and secretary of the TUC. He was elected as a Lib-Lab MP in 1885.

RITUALS

Although there are significant differences in the perspectives and roles of all three types of fraternal bodies, there have been similarities in terms of rituals and symbols across all three types of organisation. The Tolpuddle labourers were employing rituals that would have been familiar to many other men. The fraternal bodies all learned from each other and sought to support members. To do this they needed to be clear who was a member. Rituals and passwords which only members knew were developed. These enabled members to travel to other lodges and be welcomed and they often helped members to bond with one another. The initiation rites and stories that the fraternal bodies used in rituals emphasised their values, often involving oaths, blindfolding and reminders of death. Many held feasts, processions and insisted that members wore badges, sashes or regalia which identified their rank and status. In the late nineteenth century all new members of the Associated

Blacksmiths' Forge and Smithy Workers Society were told how Solomon had honoured the smiths. Members of the London Carmen's Trade Union, established in 1888 and now part of Unite, wore a sash. There is an example of the one presented to H. Crump with the insignia of the London Carmen's Trade Union and an 'all-seeing-eye' in the TUC Library Collections at the London Metropolitan University, see: http://www.unionhistory.info/timeline/Tl_Display.php?irn=3000068&QueryPage=..%2FAdvSearch.php.

When a candidate was elected to the boilermakers' union he would have to stand before the officers, the President, the Past President, the Secretary, the Sick Stewards, the Treasurer and the Doorkeepers all in sashes and regalia. The initiate then received a linen apron with the society's crest on it and the secret password and signs. To gain entry to subsequent meetings he had to give the outer guard the password and then knock on the inner door to be admitted by the inner guard. Both guards wore the sashes of office. The ritual dates from at least 1839, was revised in 1852 and an account of experiencing initiation into the boilermakers in 1912 appears in Harry Pollitt's 1940 autobiography, *Serving my time*.

Although organisations for collective action were on the edges of legality, there is evidence of semi-formal and formal bargaining among Macclesfield silk spinners, in the Coventry ribbon trade and among the Staffordshire potters. There is also considerable ritual and theatre in which the participants played out different roles. Negotiation involved an appreciation of mutual obligations, rules, petitioning and resolutions. When workers had few powers, reputation and trust counted for much. Elaborate price lists and rate books composed at meetings between representatives of employers and workers ensured that wage regulation which avoided rate-cutting benefitted both sides. The *Report of the Select Committee on Combinations* (1838), local newspapers and trade-union records indicate that although there was a trade depression, high unemployment and some wage reductions, trade unions, at least those for sectional, skilled men, survived the 1830s and 1840s. They did this by focusing on promoting the immediate interests of their members. At local level, and until they were replaced in 1846, the amateur courts of requests dealt with disputes between management and labour, effectively regulating employment relations. Local participation, custom and discretion were marginalised when professional and formal county courts became more influential.

Many accounts of the 1830s and 1840s emphasise the development of radical ideas, notably Chartism (as mentioned in Chapter 6). There were efforts to develop trade-unionism. The reformer Robert Owen established the Grand National Consolidated Trades Union. It was intended as a federation of unions but it received support from only a few trades, although some 11,000 paid their dues in April 1834. Its high-point was the April 1834 demonstration held in support of the six men of Tolpuddle. Born in Wales, Owen moved to Manchester, became a successful manufacturer and then managed textile production about 25 miles from Glasgow at New Lanark Mills, Lanark, South Lanarkshire. He made numerous innovations in terms of provision for the workforce. The site is now open to the public, see: http://www.newlanark.org/visitorcentre/. His was one of several attempts to form a general trade union. It soon collapsed. Owen also tried his hand at creating friendly societies, the Association of All Classes of All Nations and the National Community Friendly Society. Despite the failures, Owen's ideas about co-operative socialism had a considerable influence on both trade-unionism and friendly societies. There is a museum dedicated to him, in Broad Street, Newtown, Wales, see: http://robert-owen-museum.org.uk. The National Co-operative Archive, https://www.archive.coop. Holyoake House, Hanover Street, Manchester, holds many Co-operative movement records and printed materials including the papers of Robert Owen.

In 1826 the Friendly Union of Mechanics was formed in Manchester. Perhaps recognising the unpopularity of trade-unionism and the popularity of friendly societies, it soon changed its name to the Journeymen Steam Engine and Machine Makers Friendly Society and became known as the Old Mechanics. It campaigned for shorter hours and higher pay and sought to restrict entry to the trade to only those with apprenticeships. It also wanted to limit the number of apprentices. The number of working hours in a day was reduced in 1836, following a strike. Although it had setbacks, following successful legal actions taken by employers, it continued to thrive. Membership grew through amalgamations, notably with the Smiths Benevolent, Sick and Burial Society. By 1851 it became the 5,000-member-strong Amalgamated Society of Engineers. The membership had doubled within a year. It organised an overtime and piecework ban and the employers countered by locking out the men from their workplaces. The struggle ended with the union weakened and for many years it focused on prudent fundraising and developing an image of respectability. Only skilled men were permitted to join. Although by this point clearly a trade union, in many ways it continued to parallel the development of the friendly societies.

During the period between 1825 and 1871 unions were semi-legal. The risk of victimisation was recognised by the Journeymen Steam Engine Makers' Society rule book of 1850, which stated: 'Any member delegated on the Society's business and on his return losing his former situation, such member shall be allowed weekly the average rate of pay in the town or district where he resides until he finds employment.' Those who were dismissed sometimes found it hard to prove that they had been on union business and that this was the reason for the dismissal. Unions were authorised to negotiate about wages and hours but subject to numerous threats. They were not proscribed organisations, as they had been between 1799 and 1824, but neither were they as privileged and protected as unions became in the period 1871–1971. Some bodies that behaved as unions called themselves friendly societies as until 1871 the legal status of trade unions was limited. For example, in 1867 a court found that unions were not entitled to the legal remedies available to friendly societies for recovery of stolen funds. After 1871 unions negotiated about wages and conditions of work. Trade-unionism became widespread.

In 1851, the Amalgamated Society of Engineers, Machinists, Smiths, Millwrights and Pattern-makers (ASE) was created. An amalgamation of the Journeymen Steam Engine, Machine Makers' and Millwrights' Friendly Society, the Smiths Benevolent, Sick and Burial Society and a number of smaller organisations, it was open to men who had completed their apprenticeships, it eschewed initiation rites, was highly centralised and, as it charged a shilling a week, was relatively wealthy. It promoted respectability and steady growth. Almost as soon as it was formed, its 5,000 members were plunged into a lengthy and costly dispute. Although the union lost the struggle, the ASE became the model for skilled male unions. In 1859–60 when the London builders struck for the 9-hour day, the ASE donated £3,000 to the strike fund. The Amalgamated Society of Carpenters and Joiners (ASCJ) soon followed. It too had a full-time secretary, sought to avoid strike action and tried to influence legislators. In 1860 it introduced a system of static as opposed to tramp relief for its out-of-work members. In 1864–5 Robert Applegarth, its self-made secretary, intervened personally to prevent local societies in Birmingham from striking. From 1857 the text used by the President of the Boilermakers' Society when addressing candidates reminded them that 'We are united not to set class against class but to teach one another that all are brothers'. The influential historians, Beatrice and Sidney Webb, referred to these efficient, respectable, and peace-loving bodies as 'new model' unions but also noted that they were 'primarily national friendly societies'. Many trade unions provided a variety of welfare benefits including unemployment benefit. The ASCJ also offered a grant to members who wanted to emigrate to the Empire. The union sought to keep wages high and to control the supply of labour, specifically the number of apprentices. As the number of these cautious, centralised unions grew, the leaders took to meeting and lobbying together. A number became active in the Liberal Party. Biographical notes about the full-time officials of the ASCJ between 1862 and 1939 can be found on the Trade Union Ancestors website in the section on the Amalgamated Society of Woodworkers at: http://www.unionancestors.co.uk/amalgamated-society-of-wood workers/.

While Freemasons provided funds and support for members going through lean times, this was not on the formal basis of the right to payments. Friendly societies and unions institutionalised payments in times of hardship and also offered charity. In the 1860s, an ordinary family income might be between 20*s.* and 40*s.* a week. Many families found that a weekly contribution to a friendly society of about sixpence was what they could afford. Members of the bigger friendly societies, the Affiliated Orders, made payments based on age. There were increased fees for older members who were more likely to be recipients of payments. The weekly fee, depending on age, was about fourpence to eightpence a week. The benefit received was about 9*s.* a week for the first twelve months' sickness and 4*s.* 6*d.* thereafter. There was a death benefit of £9 on the death of a member and 14*s.* 6*d.* was paid out on the death of a member's wife. The ASE and the ASCJ offered more generous payments, which could not be sustained in the long run as they included pensions.

In the 1850s and 1860s trades councils were formed in Edinburgh, Glasgow, Sheffield Liverpool and London. In 1868 the first congress of the Trades Union Congress was convened by the Manchester and Salford Trades Council. The unions kept records of payments made, membership and the value of their assets. In 1867 the franchise was extended to some working men. Recognising that MPs had to gain the votes of working men, the TUC's Parliamentary Committee was formed in 1871. This was the forerunner of the General Council. There was greater interest in trade unions with a

Royal Commission on Trade Unions in 1867 and one on Labour Laws appointed in 1874. Unions presented detailed figures to Royal Commissions and other inquiries and you can access this data. The Trade Union Act of 1871 recognised unions as legal entities, as corporations and as such they were entitled to protection under the law. This reversed a court decision of 1867 when the Boilermakers had lost a case involving the embezzlement of funds. As a result, unions' funds appeared to be unprotected by the law. The 1874 Factory Act set a 10-hour limit on the working day. The Conspiracy and Protection of Property Act of 1875 offered greater status to trade unions. The Employers and Workmen Act 1875 enabled employers as well as workers to be sued for breach of contract. Although picketing was criminalised in 1871, it was decriminalised in 1875. Unions started to stand candidates for Parliament and in local elections, often working with Liberal support. Candidates representing 'Labour', there was no Labour Party until 1900, were elected in 1874 and a Labour Representation Committee was formed to support further representation.

It might be that your ancestor rose to prominence within the trade-union movement. This was a period when, increasingly, working men started to rise to positions of prominence. There was greater acceptance and integration. One such figure was Henry Broadhurst. He sat in the Commons as a Lib-Lab MP, 1880–1906. He had previously worked full-time for the Stonemasons Union, acted as a delegate to the TUC and been secretary of the Labour Representation Committee. The archives of the Labour Representation League are held at the London School of Economics. As an MP Broadhurst promoted legislation to permit working men to become JPs and for all government contracts to include a 'fair wage' clause. He later became a junior Minister and sat on two Royal Commissions. His papers are held at the London School of Economics, see: https://archives.lse.ac.uk/Record.aspx?src=Calm View.Catalog&id=BROADHURST&pos=1. He exemplifies how trade-unionists were able to gain status and respectability within the mainstream political system. If your ancestor was significantly involved in trade-union activity, you could see if there is an entry in the multi-volume *Dictionary of Labour Biography*, which is mentioned in Chapter 3.

Harry Snell, 1865–1944, started working on a farm aged 8. He became full-time aged 12 and then took a variety of jobs. He became a Unitarian and, through this connection got a job as a clerk in London. He worked for the election of the trade-unionist John Burns to the Commons in 1885. The papers of John Burns are held at the London Metropolitan University. There is also a Burns collection at the University of London Senate House Library. Snell was active in supporting strikes in 1888 and 1889. He became a county councillor then an MP and, in 1931 a peer. He eventually became Labour's Leader in the Lords and a Companion of Honour. In 1936 he wrote an autobiography, *Men, movements and myself*. Some papers relating to him are held at the Labour History Archive and Study Centre, Manchester, see: http://www.phm.org.uk/archive-study-centre/.

James Henry Thomas, 1874–1949, was illegitimate, left school aged 12 and rose to become General Secretary of the National Union of Railwaymen, 1916–31. He served as a local councillor and then as a Labour, later National Labour, MP and minister, 1910–36. He once argued that 'a Constitution which enables an engine-cleaner of yesterday to be a Secretary of State today is a great Constitution'. The titles of the autobiographies of George Barnes of the ASE, *From Workshop to War Cabinet* (1924), and of John Hodge (who in 1885 helped to found of the British Steel Smelters' Association), *From Workman's Cottage to Windsor Castle* (1931), also indicate the changes which were occurring for some trade-unionists. Less compromising is the title of Will Thorne's account, *My life's battles*, which was first published in 1925 and has been republished since. One of the founders of the National Union of Gas Workers and General Labourers, Thorne was taught to read by Karl Marx's daughter, Eleanor, and became an MP, 1918–45.

Attempts to organise unions for workers who were not classified as skilled were made. The National Agricultural Labourers' and Rural Workers' Union was formed in 1872 and recruited widely. It called for a working day of no more than 9½ hours, a minimum wage of 16s. a week and support for emigration. Employers made a concerted effort to defeat it and numbers fell. It continued to exist and enjoyed a revival in 1890 when there was a wave of unionisation among the unskilled. However, it enjoyed little success and was dissolved in 1896. Its rule book can be found in the Museum of English Rural Life, which also holds the records of other agricultural workers' unions. Some of the records of the Oxfordshire District are held in Nuffield College Library, Oxford, see: https://www.nuffield.ox.ac.uk/the-college/library/.

In 1888 a three-week strike by women making matches in east London led to the formation of the Union of Women Match Makers and a successful outcome for the workers. The following year there was a successful strike by unskilled dock labourers in east London and a massive strike by gas workers in south London. Between 1886 and 1896 the number of women trade-unionists increased from 37,000 to 118,000. In 1888 the TUC agreed that, 'where women do the same work as men they shall receive equal pay'. Membership of unions for unskilled workers grew and then rapidly fell. Nevertheless, unions for warehousemen, postmen and others developed and ones for railway clerks and shop assistants also became popular. In 1904 the Association of Shorthand Writers and Typists was formed. These bodies began to gain status and threatened the dominance of the union movement by skilled men.

With over 130 photographs, Janice Anderson's *Working Life in Britain. 1900 to 1950* (2007) provides a fascinating overview of work in the first half of the twentieth century. A deeper framework is provided in Alastair Reid's *United we stand: a history of Britain's trade unions* (2005). During the years 1900–20 the percentage of trade-union members grew from about 10 per cent of working people to almost 40 per cent, but this was not a smooth increase. In 1901 the Amalgamated Society of Railway Servants, founded in 1872, won a strike against the Taff Vale Railway Company. However, the company then sued the union for damages and won. The case went to the House of Lords where the union was held liable for damages resulting from actions by its officials and the company was awarded £23,000-plus costs. The effect was to make industrial action almost impossible and the unions swiftly turned towards Parliament to restore the unions' immunities. The Trades Disputes Act of 1906 and the unions recognised the benefits of greater representation in the Commons. Some started to support the newly formed Labour Party, but a further court case, by a Liberal in the Amalgamated Society of Railway Servants, led to a ruling that unions could not compel members to make payments to specific political parties. The period 1911–12 was one of union militancy with something like 40 million days lost to strike action. There were strikes by railway workers, transport workers and miners. The rate of trade-union growth was less during the First World War than in the period 1910–13, but it was still the case that in Britain during the war the number of trade-union members doubled. There are many records of the Amalgamated Society of Railway Servants held at the Modern Records Centre and there is online advice about these records at: https://warwick.ac.uk/services/library/mrc/explorefurther/subject_guides/family_history/rail/asrs/.

FROM 1914
When the First World War broke out in 1914 the trade-union leadership was supportive of the British government's efforts to fight the war. However, when firms with war contracts began to press to amend the agreements which preserved some work for skilled men the unions were suspicious. An agreement was made in 1915 that unskilled workers could do jobs previously reserved for skilled men, but that this change would only be for wartime. The agreement was not met with approval by all workers and there were strikes in defiance of it. The Munitions of War Act gave the government greater powers. When the South Wales miners rejected a pay offer their

> **STRIKE!**
> ON THE
> **Taff Vale Railway.**
>
> Men's Headquarters,
> Cobourn Street,
> Cathays.
>
> There has been a strike on the Taff Vale Railway since Monday last. The Management are using every means to decoy men here who they employ for the purpose of black-legging the men on strike.
>
> **Drivers, Firemen, Guards, Brakesmen, and SIGNALMEN, are all out.**
>
> Are you willing to be known as a
>
> **Blackleg?**
>
> If you accept employment on the Taff Vale, that is what you will be known by. On arriving at Cardiff, call at the above address, where you can get information and assistance.
>
> **RICHARD BELL,**
> General Secretary.

This poster was produced by the Amalgamated Society of Railway Servants during a dispute in 1900. A strike occurred after a worker was, the union argued, mistreated by his employer, the Taff Vale Railway Company. Some workers sabotaged company property by greasing the rails and uncoupling carriages. The railway company settled the matter with the union and then sued the union for damages and won. Prior to this trade unions had not been sued and the decision, which was confirmed by the House of Lords, led many trade-unionists to support campaigns for representation in Parliament. The decision was a significant factor in the formation of the Labour Party. (Crown Copyright, The National Archives, RAIL 1057/2854) proposed strike was declared illegal. However, when 200,000 miners came out the government negotiated a settlement. The Defence of the Realm Act 1914 provided the government with a range of controls over people's lives, conscription and a system of strict controls over those workers who were not conscripted were introduced and some powers, notably strike-breaking powers, were not relinquished after the war.

Co-operation between employers, unions and the government increased with unions gaining greater status and some leaders serving in government posts. Women began to join unions in greater numbers. Approximately 13 per cent of women had paid work outside the home. A few unions for white-blouse workers were created. The all-female National Federation of Women Workers was started in 1906 following the merger of a number of smaller unions. It, in turn, merged with a union that included men in 1921. The NFWW's General Secretary was Mary Macarthur who, although an opponent of the war, became secretary of the Ministry of Labour's central committee on women's employment. She had previously been the secretary of the Women's Trade Union League, which formed the basis of the women's section of the TUC. During the First World War the NFWW probably represented 10 per cent of organised women and in 1916 it secured a pay award from the Munitions Tribunal for 8,000 women in north-east England. When the government did not grant the firm the authority to pay the women, the women sat before the machines, knitting socks for soldiers. Within 24 hours the government authorised payments and work resumed. By 1918 there were a million women in trade unions, 17 per cent of the total union membership.

More workers went on strike in 1919 than in any other year of the century except 1926 and 1962. The actions of 2.4 million people led to 35 million days lost to strikes, compared with 6 million in 1918 and 11.5 million in 1913. There were more stoppages in 1920 than in any year until 1943, in mining, and until 1967, outside mining. Taking 1919 and 1920 together, 2,959 stoppages were recorded, amounting to 61,537,000 days lost to industrial action. The strikes included one across Glasgow for a 40-hour week. In Belfast over 20,000 shipyard and engineering workers held a mass meeting at which 20,225 voted for a 44-hour week and an unofficial strike to get it. By the end of the war many workers wanted more leisure time and improved living standards rather than a higher income. Before the war the standard working week was 54 hours. Unions in the shipbuilding and engineering trades had negotiated for a 47-hour week for men from 1919. While the number of hours worked fell, this was not accompanied by a fall in money wages. However, due to wartime shortages and controls (notably following the introduction in 1917 of rationing) there was a build-up of frustrated demand for goods, not political change. There was also a strike by 150,000 miners in Yorkshire for four weeks. Royal Navy stokers were sent to pump out the coal mines. The government ordered the tanks onto the streets of Glasgow to deal with a mass strike. Churchill, who had just become the Secretary of State for War and the Secretary of State for Air, called for the troops to be used to defeat a strike by electrical engineers in February 1919. In August 1919 the police went on strike with over 50 per cent of the Liverpool and Birkenhead force on strike and 75 per cent of the police in Bootle. There were four days of looting and rioting in Liverpool. The response was to send a battleship and two destroyers to be moored in the Mersey and to place tanks on the streets. At the same time in Lancashire there was also a bakers' strike, a tram drivers' strike and a call, by the local Labour Party, for a local general strike. In addition, over 450,000 cotton workers were out for 18 days and there was a national railway strike in September. On the events of that year see Simon Fowler and Daniel Weinbren's *Now the War is Over: Britain 1919–1920* (2018).

After the war many men did not want competition for paid work from women. A wartime agreement that women should not compete for post-Armistice jobs was enforced. Women largely ceased to work on the buses and trams and the 1,080 in the Women's Police Service were reduced to a few hundred. By April 1919 there were 600,000 women registered as unemployed. Although the Manchester and Salford Women's Trades Council encouraged the formation of the Domestic Workers Union of Manchester and District, there was little support, it was in competition for members with other unions and it did not thrive. Faced with unequal pay, married women being barred from some work and little in the way of union representation, women workers had to adjust to a world in which motherhood and domesticity were idealised and promoted. Many trades put their work forces on short-time and women who had worked in munitions or other industries were not permitted to register as unemployed as their 'normal' occupation was deemed to be housework. If your ancestor was resentful at working as a servant in the 1920s, the press is a good place to find reports of women workers expressing their bitterness at being offered poorly paid domestic service.

In May 1920, with the support of the TUC's Council of Action, and in order to prevent a war with the Soviet Union over Poland, dockers and stevedores of London refused to load arms and ammunition on to a vessel, the *Jolly George*, which was destined for anti-USSR forces in Poland. This was an overtly political act by the unions but the action was not illegal and the Council was sufficiently reputable that its deputation met the prime minister. In general, across the trade-union movement, the end of the war saw continuity of organisation, leadership and personnel at all levels. In many areas there was coherent policy and Labour leaders continued to argue against political strikes. While the trade disputes across the United Kingdom often had specific local causes, in Ireland nationalism was a unifying factor. After the war there was an exceptionally high level of industrial unrest in Ireland. Trade-union membership boomed and the Irish Trades Union Congress grew from 111,000 in 1914 to 300,000 in 1921. The number of days lost through strikes averaged 200,000 in the period 1914–16, 700,000 in 1917 and 1918 and 1.4 million in 1920. In Belfast alone 750,000 workdays were lost in 1919 to industrial action. In April 1918, there was a widely supported one-day general strike against conscription in Ireland and almost every town in Ireland experienced its own general strike. In January 1919, in Bagnelstown, a general strike led to the proclamation of a Provisional Soviet Government. In April 1919, Limerick Trades Council called a general strike which lasted a week. The organisers set prices and wages, issued money and set up a police force. As many as 100,000 workers claimed to have taken the day off work to celebrate May Day 1919. In June 1919, following a lock-out of 2,700 labourers in Meath and Kildare, crops were destroyed, hiring fairs disrupted and there were bayonet and baton charges against the workers. When 400 soldiers ensured the transport of cattle to Belfast, union members refused to handle the animals, which had to be returned. In July 1919 2,500 trade-unionists struck against 1,100 employers, sabotaging crops, livestock, auctions and hiring fairs. In November, 300 labourers fought 120 Royal Irish Constabulary officers in the 'Battle of Fenor' in County Waterford. There were 233 strikes in 1920, 4 times as many as during the war, including a 2-day national general strike in Ireland, demanding the release of prisoners. A strike of Cork harbour workers shut down the harbour and Dublin dock workers refused to export food to Britain. Between May and December 1920 railway workers boycotted moving British troops and military supplies in Ireland. Across the rest of Britain engagement by unions in overt political action was less commonplace.

Following the Russian Revolution of October 1917 there were claims that a soviet (that is a council of workers and soldiers) had been formed at the government-run Motor Repair Depot in Slough. One of those involved was unemployed toolmaker and member of the British Socialist Party (the Communist Party was not founded until 1920) Wal Hannington. He was one of several left-wingers who applied to work at the plant in October 1919 and soon started to run dinner hour lectures. Elected as a union official, he helped to organise a three-day strike which led to negotiations in Whitehall. Feeling victorious, Hannington returned to Slough where:

> A tremendous mass meeting was called in the chassis shop and, from a lorry used as a platform, we reported our negotiations in Whitehall. The terms of settlement were unanimously endorsed by the men, and that night as an expression of their solidarity they formed up in marching formation and marched in a body to the railway siding and the depot exits. Next morning work was resumed.

The description is of orderly collective action. The Motor Repair Depot handled lorries from the war and in April 1920 it was deemed to no longer be necessary, it was a 'white elephant'. On the last day of work a huge wooden elephant, made on the site, was ceremonially buried with a mock funeral service which concluded with a rendition of the 'Red Flag'. The Home Secretary was asked by the Conservative MP for Newcastle upon Tyne North, Nicholas Grattan-Doyle, 'whether he is in a position to give the number of Soviet committees established in South Wales, in Glasgow and Scotland generally, and the industrial centres of England; if there are very strong bodies of the same at Slough Motor Depôt'. Edward Shortt replied: 'There are, or were, a few extremists employed at Slough, but they could not be described as constituting a Soviet'. While the actions at the plant may have disrupted work there, a mock funeral on the last day cannot be classified as revolutionary in the traditions of Lenin.

By contrast, in Ireland in the years immediately prior to independence in 1921, workers used the strike weapon but also seized property and goods. The demand for land was linked to national identity and focused on ownership, not the right to be tenants. Approximately 100 soviets were established, but many collapsed when the officially recognised managers and owners made concessions to the workers. There were land seizures in County Clare, in Ballyneety, in Broadford, County Limerick and of a fishery in Castleconnell. Workers at the mills and creameries at Quartertown, Ireland, seized the plants, formed themselves into a

> **GREAT WESTERN RAILWAY.**
>
> **NOTICE TO THE STAFF.**
>
> The National Union of Railwaymen have intimated that railwaymen have been asked to strike without notice to-morrow night. Each Great Western man has to decide his course of action, but I appeal to all of you to hesitate before you break your contracts of service with the old Company, before you inflict grave injury upon the Railway Industry, and before you arouse ill feeling in the Railway service which will take years to remove.
>
> Railway Companies and Railwaymen have demonstrated that they can settle their disputes by direct negotiations. The Mining Industry should be advised to do the same.
>
> Remember that your means of living and your personal interests are involved, and that Great Western men are trusted to be loyal to their conditions of service in the same manner as they expect the Company to carry out their obligations and agreements.
>
> FELIX J. C. POLE,
> General Manager.
>
> PADDINGTON STATION,
> May 2nd, 1926.

The General Strike began at midnight on 3 May 1926. Immediately prior its start, this appeal is dated 2 May, the Great Western Railway Company called for the workforce to be 'loyal to their conditions of service'. This document is in The National Archives, Kew, which houses many documents relevant for historians of the trade-union movement. (Crown Copyright The National Archives, RAIL 253/451)

workers' council and ran production. At Mungret labourers demanded that a large estate's lands be divided among them. In May 1920 workers in Knocklong creameries made deals with farmers and suppliers, declared a soviet and operated under the slogan: 'We make butter not profits'. They won a pay rise, shorter hours and the removal of an unpopular manager. The miners took over the Arigna coal mine in County Leitrim and ran it as a soviet for two months before the workers got a pay rise and handed back the mine to its owners. In Dublin and Drogheda 700 engineers took over their foundry and proclaimed a soviet which lasted six weeks. Two flour mills in Cork were seized by their employees. A gasworks in Waterford was run under workers' control for six weeks and the Tipperary gas workers created their own soviet and the town coachworks became a soviet, as did the Monaghan mental hospital. Unemployed workers took over and reopened a closed sawmill in Ballinacourty. In Cleeves factory, Limerick (Ireland's fifth largest city), a soviet was established. A bakery and mills in Bruree, County Limerick, were occupied for a month by employees. When creamery owners attempted to cut wages by one-third, almost a hundred creameries were turned into soviets. There was the appropriation of mills, creameries, factories and later railways and docks and land by workers in Cork. Following an attempt to increase the hours of railway staff, the workers took control and, for two days, ran the railways.

The wave of disruption after the war faded as concessions were made to trade unions. The mines were taken under direct government control during the war, wages rose and the union favoured continued public ownership. After the war the mines were returned to private ownership, and wages fell. The miners arranged to go on strike in co-ordination with the rail and transport workers but the other two unions backed down and the miners went on strike alone. In 1925 wages were again cut. The government subsidised wages for nine months, until 1 May 1926. The owners locked the miners out of the pits until the workforce agreed to lower wages. The government declared a state of emergency and workers in key industries were called out on strike by the TUC. An estimated 2.5 million people went on strike. The government used the army and volunteers to maintain essential services. Royal Navy submarines were moved to the London docks to provide electricity from their batteries for the meat store. Many of the latter strikebreakers were in the Organisation for the Maintenance of Supplies, which, Hackney striker Julius Jacobs recalled, was known as the Organisation of Mugs and Scabs. This recollection can be found in Jeffrey Skelley's *The General Strike* (1976). After nine days (3–12 May), the TUC, which had been holding secret talks with the mine owners, called off the strike. It had won no concessions and the miners stayed out on strike. Local Labour parties ran a soup kitchen and raised money. Adoption schemes to help miners' children were established. Union membership fell. By the end of November most men were back down the mines, working for less pay and longer hours. Bill Carr was an 18-year-old miner in Newcastle when the strike broke out. He recalled that at the end of the lock-out 'none of my family were accepted when they presented themselves for work. Yet the family – my grandfather, father and I – had worked in the industry for a total of 110 years, (grandfather first went down the pit at the age of eleven)'. Skelley noted that Bill Carr went on: 'On November 29, it was all over, The lockout had lasted seven months and things would never be the same again'. There are also recollections of the strike in Daniel Weinbren's *Generating Socialism: Recollections of Life in the Labour Party* (1997) and Robert Leeson's *Strike: a live history: 1887–1971* (1973). As a result of this strike and others, many workers lost their jobs during the interwar period. In 1926 the Manchester District of the engineers' union, which had developed from the Steam Engine Makers' Society, established a 'Shop Stewards' Victimisation Fund. One case it dealt with was that of Amalgamated Engineering Union Shop Steward Vic Parker, who was dismissed in 1939. He explained that the company director had written two letters, one to Vic suggesting that there was a shortage of work and that was the reason for the dismissal. The other to the General Manager. Vic later wrote that this latter letter was: 'to say I was a dangerous Red and must be got rid of at any cost. Unfortunately or fortunately the letters were placed in the wrong envelopes and I received the letter intended for the General Manager'.

Following the General Strike, legislation passed by a Conservative government outlawed sympathetic strikes and made other forms of action illegal. Some civil servants were forbidden to join unions affiliated to the TUC and instead of a percentage of affiliated union members' dues going to the Labour Party by default, members had to direct their money to Labour. The funding of the party fell but union leaders strengthened their commitment to the party as the means by which the law could be changed. In 1928 the unions contributed most of Labour's money, most of its MPs and ten times as many members as those who had joined on an individual basis. Ernest Bevin, the General Secretary of the Transport and General Workers' Union, and Walter Citrine, the Secretary of the TUC Council, were particularly influential within the Labour Party. The papers of the Transport and General Workers' Union are held at the Modern Record Centre, https://archiveshub.jisc.ac.uk/search/archives/71921329-c335-3f3e-927a-468aca203805.

During the late 1920s and through the 1930s legislation and high levels of unemployment had the effect of reducing the membership of unions and their powers. The unions tended to focus more on conciliation and industrial concerns. Several unions merged to form vast, general unions. There were over 1,300 unions in 1900 and fewer than 800 by 1945. Nevertheless, there were unions that did not conform to this pattern. In 1929 the Communist Party, having worked with the wider labour movement since the party's foundation in 1920, took the view that the Labour Party and the trade unions were strike-breaking instruments and that the Communists needed to establish new trade unions. One of these was for clothing workers and there was soon a strike. For materials on left-wing political activists try the Marx Memorial Library & Workers' School, 37a Clerkenwell Green London EC1R 0DU, 020 7253 1485, https://www. marx-memorial-library.org. Here there are over 50,000 books and pamphlets including material on some unions and friendly societies and the wider working-class movement.

Songs for strikers were a popular idea. The tune of 'Tramp, Tramp, Tramp', a song from the American Civil War, was used by London dockers during their strike of 1889. The verses explained the case for paying a 'tanner [sixpence] on the hour' and the desperation for work of the throng at the dock gates, while the chorus reiterated the method required for change: 'Strike, boys, strike for better wages, Strike, boys, strike for better pay, Go on fighting at the docks, Stick it out like fighting cocks, Go on fighting til the bosses they give way'. According to Mary Brooksbank, 1897–1980, a jute mill worker, another version was used in 1912 in Dundee: 'We are out for higher wages as we have a right to do, An' we'll never be content till we get oor ten per cent, For we have a right tae live as well as you.'

In Belfast in 1874 the local newspaper reported women involved in one of the earliest and largest industrial strikes in Ireland: 'found their chief delight in going about in bands, singing snatches of popular songs, after a style and fashion peculiarly their own'. The same newspaper reported a strike of spinners in Belfast in 1906 and that the female participants marched through the 'main thoroughfares of the city, singing and shouting'. Women workers from Bryant and May of east London marched to songs while on strike in 1889. In 1918 or 1919 the National Agricultural Labourers' and Rural Workers' Union produced a *Songbook*. There is a copy in the Norfolk and Norwich Record Office. In the 1920s an estimated 250,000 Londoners went to Kent each year to harvest hops. The workers, predominantly women, frequently organised strikes over pay. They also sang, in Yiddish and English, as they worked. Some of the song lyrics called upon fellow hoppers not to accept a poor piece rate and to fight for a fair measurement of the hops picked. If you interview an ancestor who was a union member, don't forget to ask them to sing you any strike songs they recall.

STRIKE SONGS

In 1929 the Communist Party produced *Rego and Polikoff strike songs*. This book of thirty-five strike songs connected two recent stoppages: at Rego's, Edmonton, and at Polikoff's, Hackney. Both strikes were in the garments trade and involved women workers. For Communists, marginalised in the mainstream media, the booklet could raise funds, aid recruitment and support retention. The songs indicate how the writers, and the singers, promoted a particular view of the world. They represented the past in a way that explained the present. The strikes were not very successful but defeat was represented as defiance and a dream of a victory deferred. Singing enabled working women to disrupt, assert themselves and to claim the streets as their own space while mocking the employers who had 'got their brains at the wrong end'. These parodies of popular songs emphasised the issues central to the strikers. In the strike-song booklet, the lyrics included: 'We had to travel further, Our work they made it harder, More work! Less pay!' and 'We won't give way, til they increase our pay'. The songs might also have raised spirits: 'The Rego Girls are marching with spirits all aglow . . . Whizz bang rah! Who the hell d'ye think we are? Strikers!' Whereas the strikers were 'bonnie', the strikebreakers were 'dirty blacklegs', 'skunks' and 'scabs'. There were reminders of the benefits of union membership with the lines: 'We'll still march under our union banner triumphantly' and 'We will all support our leaders who are going to pull us through'. The London based strikers were opposed by the employers and the mainstream trade union which was based in Leeds. There are several cockney terms in the lyrics such as the rhyming slang for money 'bread', i.e. bread and honey equals money. If your ancestor worked in the East End clothing trade, the chances of you hearing her voice are slim. However, songs such as these can tell you a bit more about why she joined a trade union, why she remained a member for so long and a bit about the fun she had.

Between the wars the unemployed gathered to march to London to draw attention to their plight. There were hunger marches in 1922–3, and a larger one followed in 1932. Organised by the National Unemployed Workers' Movement, some 2,000 to 3,000 people in 18 contingents converged on London. There were further marches in 1934 and 1936. Many trades councils, co-operatives, local Labour parties and trade-unionists supported the marchers and provided help. Trade-unionists were also involved in anti-fascist activities. Over £2 million worth of clothing, food and supplies was sent to the Republicans in Spain, where fascists were attempting to seize power from the elected Republican government. Some trade-unionists also volunteered to fight and help the wounded in Spain. There were also a number of fights and campaigns against the British Union of Fascists. Trade-unionists were often involved. The fascists wanted trade unions to be preserved within a fascist corporate structure, with a different leadership and unable to take strike action.

Personal accounts of trade-unionism between the wars gives a flavour of how it was about more than negotiations over wages and conditions. While some shop stewards were in favour of agitation for improvements, an important strand of trade-unionism was represented by people such as Sam Ratcliffe, a United Machine Workers' Association member at the Metropolitan-Vickers works in Trafford Park, Manchester. He became the Chair of the workers' side of the Works' Committee which was established in 1917, and retained that position until 1942. He was also shop stewards' representative on the Manchester District Committee of the AEU until 1939 and was associated with running the Works' Benevolent Fund, the Long Service Association and the Motor Vehicle Club. The historian of the Metropolitan-Vickers Electrical Co., 1899–1949, John Dummelow, concluded of Ratcliffe that 'few have made a greater contribution to the smooth running of the works'.

After the Nottinghamshire Miners' Association negotiated its own deal with managers, in defiance of the national miners' strike of 1926, a breakaway, the Nottinghamshire and District Miners'

Industrial Union, was formed. Members went to Wales to break strikes. They were defeated by a series of underground sit-ins in 1934. The breakaway lasted 11 years. Dick Martin, a Nottinghamshire miner, argued that their collaboration with management was effective. He is quoted in a well-illustrated BBC book, Peter Pagnamenta and Richard Overy's *All our working lives* (1984), a collection based on personal memories of workers:

> We had union men that weren't militant . . . most of our union men at that time would try to make a pal of gaffers. So, if you wanted something from the manager you could go and say, 'Well, couldn't we do anything for so-and-so because he's not a bad bloke, y'know' and they got more out of the gaffer like that . . . That's why we got better paid than Wales and north-east.

In the case of Evan Williams, the Chair of the South Wales Coal Owners' Association, making 'a pal of the gaffers' may not have been easy. Foster Lewis recalled one set of negotiations when Williams merely shook his head at all the arguments and evidence put by the union: 'He just shook his head. So not a word was spoken by the coal-owners' representative.'

Some trade-union leaders worked with employers to marginalise militant elements. In 1919 Conservative MP Reginald Hall together with a group of industrialists founded National Propaganda. It soon became the Economic League, keeping track of left-wing organisations and individuals, with material supplied by spies within unions and from police files. In addition, it organised meetings and distributed leaflets. Active in the 1920s and 1930s, after the Second World War it became more secretive but continued to keep a blacklist of people employers might wish to avoid employing. Throughout the 1960s and 1970s it was funded by a number of companies and it denied the accuracy of newspaper reports about its blacklist. In 1988 a television report claimed that it had received information from within the ASTMS for over twenty years. There were also reports on the inaccuracy of the records it held. The number of subscribers fell. It continued to claim that it had good relations with a number of trade-union leaders. In 1990, the House of Commons Select Committee on Employment took evidence from the Economic League about its blacklist and extracts were published in the *Daily Mirror*. You might find an ancestor's name in these records. It closed in 1993 but a new body, the Consulting Association, took over its blacklist role. Once information about this database became widely known following a series of court cases, the organisation had to pay compensation and was formally closed in 2009. As with its predecessors, it relied upon informers within the police and the trade unions. Court cases have continued following accusations of further illegal vetting procedures.

A useful source for getting a flavour of how unions have operated and thrived between the wars is by taking a look at their own informal publications. Shop stewards have long produced handouts, leaflets and news sheets. In September 1913, *Solidarity*, 'a monthly journal of militant trade unionism', was distributed by engineering trades shop stewards. After a few issues it ceased but in 1916 it reappeared as *Solidarity*, 'a journal of modern trade unionism'. It featured discussions about the value of the shop stewards' movement, poetry and appeals for funds. It reported on strikes and campaigns. In 1921 the decision was made to close it and focus on the *Worker*, 'the organ of the Clyde Workers' Committee'. This had been produced intermittently since 1916 and there were other versions of it, such as that produced by the Sheffield Workers' Committee, 1919–20. The engineers produced many other short-lived journals such as the *Engineers' Bulletin*, 1934–5, the *Conveyor*, 1937–8 and the *New Propellor* (later *Metal Worker*), 1935–62. These contained, advice, songs, news, humour, sports, educational articles, material aimed specifically at women, campaigns and correspondence. Some of these publications can be found in the Working Class Movement Library, https://www.wcml.org.uk/.

UNIONS AND COMMUNITY

Welsh coalminer Will Paynter, a Communist and trade-union activist, was elected as the checkweighman at his colliery in 1929. He noted of the post that: 'The job of checking weights was easy enough, but it also entailed advising men on union matters and giving leadership'. In 1930, following a demonstration, Paynter was imprisoned but his job as checkweighman was kept for him on his release. In 1931 he was taken to court for interfering with the management of the colliery, a breach of the 1860 Checkweighman's Act. He lost the case and his job. The miners' union permitted unemployed miners to be involved in union activity and in 1936 he was elected to the executive committee of the South Wales Miners' Federation (SWMF) and became President of the South Wales area of the National Union of Mineworkers (formerly the SWMF). When he looked back on the union for which he had worked for many years, he described the SWMF as:

> a lot more than a trade union. It was a social institution providing through its local leaders an all-round service of advice and assistance to the mining community on most of the problems that could arise between the cradle and the grave. Its function became a combination of economic, social and political leadership in these single industry communities . . . The leaders of the local miners' lodges were very much more than representatives dealing with problems of wages and conditions of employment in the mines. They were acknowledged social leaders called upon to help and advise in all kinds of domestic and social problems; they were indeed the village elders to whom people went when in any kind of trouble [. . .] I was a sort of professional letter writer especially in the village where I lived. Harassed wives who had fallen behind in hire purchase instalments on some household

goods, or had accumulated arrears of rent or any kind of debt, would require letters to be sent appealing for a stay of action by the firms involved. Many times I have appeared in the local court to testify as to the character of the man or child who had fallen foul of the law, and to appeal for leniency [. . .] It was accepted by the union official and the public that he was obliged to give this service if he could [. . .] The miners' federation were pillars of the communities because the miners' institutes and welfare halls provided places for the social and cultural activity and their domination of the local labour parties decisively influenced local politics.

The Richard Burton Archives in the Swansea University Singleton Park campus library in Swansea holds the South Wales Coalfield Collection, http://lisweb.swan.ac.uk/swcc/. This includes records of the South Wales Miners' Federation, later the NUM (South Wales Area) and its individual lodges. There are also records from miners' institutes, co-operative societies and individuals connected with the mining community. You need to book in advance if you wish to visit. See: http://www.swansea.ac.uk/library/archive-and-research-collections/richard-burton-archives/.

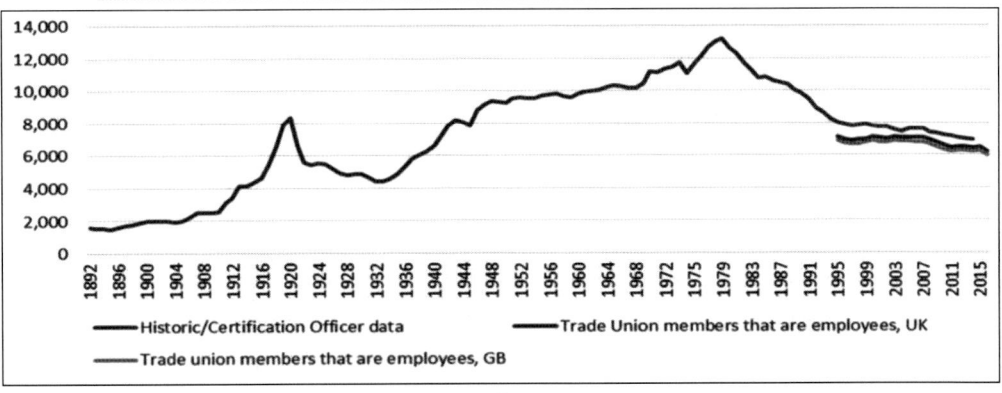

Trade-union membership levels in UK from 1892 to 2016.

SINCE THE 1940s

During the Second World War the General Secretary of the Transport and General Workers' Union, Ernest Bevin, was made Minister of Labour and National Service. Strikes were banned and Bevin could direct labour to where it was required. When miners in Kent went on strike over 1,000 of the strikers were fined and their leaders were imprisoned. Further strikes followed, as did legislation to outlaw incitement to strike. Disputes between unions arose. In 1944 the boilermakers' union insisted that only its members could operate a new flame-planing machine. There was a strike and the men were summoned and fined. Government contracts were awarded only to companies that complied with trade-union standards. Union membership rose from 6 million in 1938 (including 4.5 million affiliated to the TUC) to 7.8 million (6.7 million affiliated) in 1945. Trade unions were firmly integrated, with significant powers and responsibilities.

Many union publications appeared infrequently during the war but afterwards local union magazines started to be published. They carried cartoons and book reviews. The *Trade Union News and Tatler*, which ran 1945–7, was for shop-floor and office workers at Ferguson Pailin Ltd, an electrical engineering company based in Manchester. Ben Heap was one of the editors for the whole period:

> The Editorial Board was set up by the Shop Stewards Committee. At first Bill Derby shared the jobs out, but when we got going it was run on democratic lines. The front page always contained articles on political and topical subjects. The Board decided the subject, then two were detailed off to get on with the job. Everyone on the Board had to take their turn at writing these front page articles. Bill Derby had a column to himself, under the pseudonym 'Onlooker'. My job was to allocate space to each writer and tell them how many words they could have. I also had to look after the back page. We had many contributions from the shop floor.

Ford Worker, a monthly produced in 1949, reported on the play *The six men of Dorset*. Unusually, the *Voice*, another Ford workers' journal, produced in 1957, carried commercial advertisements. There are many names in these magazines and although some of them are noms de plume, you might find an ancestor quoted in one. However, beware that some of the material is formulaic. Often the letters of thanks follow a familiar pattern such as this one from a convenor called E. Shelland, published in August 1952: 'I would like to thank the *Metal Worker* on behalf of the Ferguson Strike Committee and all the workers at our factory for the wonderful assistance you gave us. We secured a complete victory after four weeks in dispute, including the dismissal of the blacklegs'.

In 1945, 120 newly elected, union-sponsored MPs took their seats in the Labour-dominated House of Commons. In the Cabinet of twenty, six were sponsored by unions. An important element of the post-General Strike legislation, the Trades Disputes Act 1927, was repealed. In the six years after 1945 trade-union membership rose from 7.6 million to 9.2 million. Moreover, many felt unions were of great importance. Ferdynand Zweig's *The British Worker* (1952) concluded that: 'the unions mean a great deal to the men, even those who do not bother about attending meetings or who criticise their policy or leadership. Thus being called a "blackleg" or "scab" was something no man could survive; often, the only possible option to a strikebreaker, was to leave the area.'

In his 1969 autobiography, *Good Morning, Brothers!*, dock workers' leader Jack Dash told a story that supported this research: 'I stood talking to an elderly docker, nodding a "Good morning" to another older chap as he passed. "Jack" said my old pal, "for Christ's sake don't lower yourself to talk to that no-good, dirty, blacklegging scabbing bastard!" Apparently, he had scabbed in the big strike of 1921 – and this was 1964!'

Having helped to achieve increased productivity during the Second World War and with their status further bolstered by the support of the 1945 Labour government, the trade unions appeared to be firmly embedded within the new order. However, the late 1940s also saw a series of unofficial strikes by dock workers. Unpaid convenors and shop stewards led these strikes which did not gain the support of the elected, full-time union officials.

After Labour lost power, in 1951, the unions remained close to government. They also remained cautious and moderate. Resolutions to the TUC denouncing wage restraint were voted down and when a motion was carried in 1952, against the wishes of the General Council, demanding that a list of industries be nationalised, the list that was eventually drawn up only recommended that the water supply be nationalised. When national strikes in engineering, shipbuilding and the railways were threatened, the government intervened to ensure that wages were increased. Other wages rose and the early 1950s remained relatively strike-free. It was a time when there were relatively few trade-unionists in agriculture and the clothing, food, tobacco and drink industries and some parts of the country had few members. In Dudley 12 per cent of workers were in unions and in 1951 a union study of Coventry indicated that about half of those eligible to join the Amalgamated Engineering Union were members. Only about 20 per cent of trade-unionists attended meetings and there was little else to do within unions. In 1945 the Civil Service Clerical Association Theatre Group claimed to be the only union body of its kind. Even among the miners, where, as Paynter noted, the union was said to have had a great impact outside work, studies made in the period concluded that choirs, musical clubs and dramatic societies were being spurned in favour of commercial pursuits, drinking and gambling.

There were strikes in 1955, but studies indicate that the popular view was that these were caused by the unions and that the government was not to blame. The TUC's reputation fell, and about a third of trade-unionists voted Conservative in the 1950s. By 1960 there were 9.8 million trade-unionists in Britain, a gain of ½ million over a decade. However, the proportion of trade-unionists to the total employed population had fallen from 44 per cent in the late

1940s to 41 per cent. Between 1964 and 1970 women accounted for 70 per cent of the increase in members of TUC trade unions, much of this rise being because female-dominated unions affiliated. Men, however, tended to control the leadership, even of unions where half the members were women. When recording an ancestor who you think was a union member in the 1950s you might find that their memory of union activity during the period is hazy and that they are a little embarrassed about their involvement in a union.

In 1968 the women sewing machinists, whose strike at Fords was the subject of the film *Made in Dagenham* (2010), organised a strike over unequal grading. This was done independently of the male-dominated Transport and General Workers' Union. It was not the first strike for equal pay by women workers. There was one at Rolls-Royce in Glasgow in 1943 and another at Ford Halewood which also took place in 1968. However, it was the machinists' strike that created the pressure that led to the 1970 Equal Pay Act. More women joined unions and in 1979 the TUC drew up a *Charter for Equality for Women within Trade Unions*. Unofficial action spread. A government report on industrial relations of 1968 concluded that perhaps as many as 95 per cent of all strikes were initiated without the knowledge or approval of union officials. The focus on the workshop made the work of coordinated strategic decision-making about pay or discipline more complicated as it was not clear where power lay. In the Austin Motor Company factory in Longbridge, Birmingham, workers in single workshops or departments would go on strike over local grievances and sometimes only for a few hours. Many actions involved fewer than 200 people. The factory convenor, Dick Etheridge, did not know of some disputes until the workers had left. A shift in wage structure in the early 1970s put pressure on the unions to co-ordinate across Longbridge and other factories. At some works mass meetings were held, at others there would be discussions and votes at workshop level.

Elsewhere, particularly in the public sector, the convention of negotiations at national level continued. Even though in hospitals many members were women, in the early 1970s men, who tended not to do as much as women in the home, often held elected branch positions and attended union meetings. At St Thomas' Hospital in south London, the local branch of the Confederation of Hospital Employees focused on case work in support of individual workers. Women took their problems to the male branch secretary who decided on the action to be taken. After 1971 shop stewards began to become more prominent. Many of these were elected female departmental representatives. They held local meetings and listened to members. Attendance at branch meetings rose and there was a more collective approach to grievances. In 1973, the branch organised its first strike and elected its first female branch secretary. At Longbridge de-centralised organisation and workgroup-based decision-making had become chaotic. In the case of the St Thomas' Hospital branch, where a top-down structure was replaced by devolved powers, activism increased. Power between branch and national level shifted over time as a result of individual and collective actions and also regulation and legislation.

The type of union changed as well. The cotton, mining and rail industries declined while white-collar work increased. Brian Simon's autobiographical notes are contained in a Centerprise collection, *Working Lives. Volume Two Hackney 1945–77* (1977). Simon noted that:

> 'I just couldn't imagine a union of teachers: my idea of a union was dockers or builders . . . there were a lot of teachers who wouldn't have dreamed of taking industrial action: that was something that the lower orders did'. He went out on an unofficial strike, which became official, and that 'all the teachers joined the union. We had regular union meetings and we regularly win small issues like the right to "supply teachers"'.

By 1979 about 44 per cent of all white-collar workers were in trade unions and 40 per cent of all trade-union members held white-

Gordon Wilson speaking from a Scottish Trades Union Congress (STUC) bus on the campaign to save Gartcosh Works. Scottish politician and solicitor Gordon Wilson (1938–2017) was an MP, 1974–87, and led the Scottish National Party, 1979–90. This photograph is undated but was probably taken in early 1986. The iron works at Gartcosh opened in 1865 and became a steel mill owned by the British Steel Corporation. It was closed in February 1986. The STUC is independent of the TUC, and its records are held in Glasgow Caledonian University Archives. The Scottish Political Archive is housed at the University of Stirling and is home to the oral interviews, personal papers and associated material from prominent Scottish politicians. (Scottish Political Archive, University of Stirling)

collar jobs. Public service trade unions, notably the Confederation of Health Service Employees and the National Association of Local Government Officers, enjoyed huge rises in membership.

The leaders of some large unions became critical of the 1974–9 Labour government. In his autobiography, *The Time of my life* (1990), a member of that government, Denis Healey, was critical of union activists:

Islington Trades Council banner being aired in March 2011. It is 8 x 6ft in size and cost £650. Made by Ed Hall, it was sponsored by solicitors Edwards Duthie. There are images of unnamed workers on the banner. It also refers to specific local events and individuals. Copenhagen House, Islington, was the scene in 1834 of a demonstration of 100,000 people who called for the return of the Tolpuddle Martyrs (transported to Australia in 1834). There is Vic Turner (wearing a red tie), one of the Pentonville Five. These dockers, gaoled in 1972, were supported by thousands of trade-unionists and soon released. He later became a local councillor and the mayor of Newham. Thomas Paine (1737–1809) is pictured holding his book, The rights of man, *outside the Angel pub, Islington. This is where he is said to have written it in 1792. There is a quote from the book on the banner. Islington Town Hall is shown, with a red flag flying. (© Duncan Harris)*

The Winter of Discontent was not caused by the frustration of ordinary workers after a long period of wage restraint. It was caused by institutional pressures from local trade union activists who had found their roles severely limited by three years of income policy agreed by their national leaders. . .

Trade Unions

Unfortunately, the Labour Party's financial and constitutional links with the unions made it difficult for us to draw too much attention to their role in our defeat.

It is not only autobiographies of those who were outside the trade unions that can be useful sources. Healey complained of union activists, and such activists were less successful in their campaign for Asian women workers in 1976–8. The Association of Professional and Executive, Clerical and Computer Staff was for white-collar staff. It was not led by left-wingers, indeed, in 1976 it retained its rule that Communist Party members had to declare their political affiliation when standing for election to union posts. In August 1976, when women who worked at a photograph processing plant in Willesden, north London, joined the union and immediately went on strike, it was not instantly supportive. However, by September it had declared the strike 'official'. The majority of strikers were East African Asian women. They received widespread support from the labour movement with over 500 arrests following mass picketing. There was also a refusal by the post office workers to deliver the post which was vital to the commercial success of this mail order company. The factory owner was supported by many Conservative MPs. An inquiry chaired by Lord Scarman concluded that the union should be recognised and the strikers reinstated. The owner rejected the report, the House of Lords supported the right not to recognise a union, the strikers were not reinstated and the union was not recognised. The TUC understood the necessity of acting within the legal framework but was wary of using the courts to assist in its struggles. The strikers called off their action in 1978, nearly two years after it had started. In 1978 the leader of Brent Trades Council, Jack Dromey, co-authored with Graham Taylor, wrote a book about the affair, *Grunwick, the workers story*. In 2018 the Grunwick 40 project was created by Brent Trades Council, Willesden Green Town Team and Brent Museum and Archives, and funded by the Heritage Lottery Fund, among other bodies. An exhibition and a film, *The Great*

Grunwick Strike, were also made. There are further records in the Modern Record Centre, see: http://mrc-catalogue.warwick.ac.uk/search/all:records/0_20/all/score_desc/grunwick. Also the Brent Museum and Archives, see: https://www.brent.gov.uk/services-for-residents/brent-museum-and-archives/. The Metropolitan Police records relating to this matter were released following a Freedom of Information request, see: http://specialbranchfiles.uk/grunwick-dispute-files-overview/.

In 1972 the miners went on strike, the Conservative prime minister called an election, Labour won and, after sixteen weeks on strike, the miners returned to accept a 35 per cent pay rise. Unions continued to win concessions from employers. Union membership rose further by about 3 million in the 1970s, to reach almost 13 million by 1980. During the 1980s the miners were defeated after a year-long strike and the print unions also lost out in their struggle with News International. Union membership fell and by 1997, when Labour came to power, it was down to 8 million.

This was a period when a woman came to lead a major industrial trade union, the Society of Graphical and Allied Trades (SOGAT), the membership of which included both women (40 per cent) and men. Brenda Dean started work aged 16 in 1959. She spent thirty-three years as a full-time trade-union official and in 1986–7 as General Secretary of SOGAT, leading it in a struggle with the newspaper proprietor Rupert Murdoch. The dispute led to 5,000 of her members being sacked. A 2007–8 recording of an interview about her life is part of the 'Oral History of the British Press' collection held by the British Library, https://sounds.bl.uk/Oral-history/Press-and-media/021M-C0638X0015XX-0001V0. Brenda also wrote an autobiography, *Hot Mettle: SOGAT, Murdoch and me* (2007), which focused on her time as SOGAT General Secretary.

The TUC encouraged rationalisation, mergers and amalgamations. Brenda Dean's SOGAT merged with the National Graphical Association to form the Graphical, Paper and Media Union, which in turn became part of Unite. In 1993 the National Union of Public

Employees merged with the National and Local Government Officers Association and the Confederation of Health Service Employees to form Unison. A high proportion of the full-time officials of this new union were women. By 2008 there were only 167 trade unions and since then the number has fallen. The latest data, as compiled by the government, can be found at: https://www.gov.uk/government/publications/public-list-of-active-trade-unions-official-list-and-schedule/trade-unions-the-current-list-and-schedule. Today about 6 million employees in the UK are trade-union members – there was small increase in 2013 – but the figure is well below the peak of over 13 million in 1979. The proportion of employees who were trade-union members fell to 23.5 per cent in 2016, the lowest rate of trade-union membership for many years. It was 32.4 per cent in 1995. The proportion of women who were in a trade union was around 26 per cent in 2016, compared with 21 per cent for men. Older workers account for a larger proportion of union members than younger workers. The proportion of trade-union members aged below 50 has fallen since 1995, while the proportion aged above 50 has increased. Employees in professional occupations were more likely to be trade-union members than other employees. The anti-union laws, the reduction in employment protection, the end of full employment, the extension of zero-hour contracts, the defeat of major unions and the shift in the membership of the business elite have all contributed to the decline. The rapid changes in the ownership of shares and the complexity of the long supply chain arrangements and the concentration of capital make it difficult for unions to negotiate. Although trade-union membership levels may have stabilised in recent years, the proportion of UK employees in the trade union has declined. Union membership levels have not kept pace with the increase in the total number of UK employees.

SOURCES AND COLLECTIONS

The TUC Library Collections include pamphlets and campaign materials from the Women's Trade Union League, numerous reports on union matters and some personal materials. Papers relating to the Bryant and May match workers' strike are also held at the London Metropolitan University, 16 Goulston Street, London E1 7TP, http://www.unionhistory.info/about.php, 020 7320 3516. The Trades Union Congress Library Collections are part of the Special Collections at the London Metropolitan University Library, The Wash Houses, Old Castle Street, London, http://student.londonmet.ac.uk/library/using-the-library/special-collections/trades-union-congress-library-collections/. The archive includes the personal papers of several prominent trade-unionists. There is also material about several individual unions and the London Trades Council. The *150 voices* project presents a set of trade-union stories from the past 150 years. The TUC says that these are 'snapshots of trade unionists whose stories will surprise, move and inspire you', https://tuc150.tuc.org.uk/about-tuc-150/.

As unions often operated as friendly societies union records provide not only members' names but also additional information such as their marital status and their nominee for funeral benefits. There are many examples of such registration materials at the Modern Record Centre. This is on the campus of the University of Warwick in the Central Campus Library extension, CV4 7AL. It is the main repository in Britain for the records of trade unions and employers' organisations. It holds records of the TUC, numerous national trade-union collections and papers of leading trade-unionists. Most of the material dates from the late nineteenth century onwards. It also has papers relating to the British Trotskyist movement and anarchist and libertarian groups and many personal papers, including, for example, the trade-union archives of Ernest Bevin. Note, despite the name of the university, it is situated about 10km from Warwick. The nearest station is in Coventry, 5km away. See: https://www2.warwick.ac.uk/services/library/mrc/. The universities in Swansea, Hull and London also hold potentially useful collections. The Archives Hub, https://archiveshub.jisc.ac.uk, provides information about collections held in archives in UK universities and colleges. There is also a 'free-to-use database of archives and manuscript collections from many of London's higher education institutions' at: http://www.aim25.com/index.stm. Through this you can track down some friendly society and trade-union records.

Other places that keep records of trade unions and trade-unionists include the Working Class Movement Library, 51 Crescent, Salford M5 4WX, 016 1736 3601, https://www.wcml.org.uk. This is a reference library, and you will need to make an appointment if you wish to study materials there. There are books, pamphlets, posters, journals and leaflets and a collection of audio recordings. These relate to working class lives, work and campaigns. It is strong in the area of records of trade unions and shop stewards in the north west of England and in the engineering industry. You might find it helpful to visit the family history page at: https://www.wcml.org.uk/wcml/en/our-collections/family-history/.

The Labour History Archive & Study Centre is within the People's History Museum, Left Bank, Spinningfields, Manchester, M3 3ER, 016 1838 9190, http://www.phm.org.uk/archive-study-centre/. It holds the archives of the Labour Party and the Communist Party, and personal papers of nationally important figures in the labour movement. There are also materials relating to Chartism and friendly societies. There are pamphlets, newspapers and many items about trade unions and trade-unionists.

The University of Hull archive houses the papers of prominent left-wing individuals and several national co-operative and radical organisations. It also contains many friendly society records and materials. John Saville's now rather dated *The Labour Archive at the University of Hull* was published by the Brynmor Jones Library of the University of Hull in 1989, and may be of help. You can access the catalogue at: http://www.hullhistorycentre.org.uk/home.aspx.

The People's History Museum and the Working Class Movement Library are among those places where it is pleasant to take a tour or simply look around at the exhibits. Your ancestor might have carried a banner, distributed leaflets or worn a badge such as those exhibited. On banners see Annie Ravenhill-Johnson and Paula James' *The Art and Ideology of the Trade Union Emblem, 1850–1925* (2013). There is a collection of pole-heads from banners and processional staffs at the Museum of English Rural Life, University of Reading, Redlands Road, Reading, RG1 5EX, https://merl.reading.ac.uk.

While there are not many records created by trade unions in The National Archives, there are records relating to mines and mining, see: http://www.nationalarchives.gov.uk/help-with-your-research/research-guides/mines-mining/, and railways, see: http://www.nationalarchives.gov.uk/help-with-your-research/research-guides/railways/. There are details of unions registered with the Registrar of Friendly Societies from 1870 and, from 1971, material from the Chief Registrar of Trade Unions and Employers Associations. The LAB 2 series relates to the Ministry of Labour and its predecessors, see: http://discovery.nationalarchives.gov.uk/details/r/C10117. Through the catalogue information on industrial relations, women's equality rights, labour disputes, working hours and health and safety issues can be found, see: http://discovery.nationalarchives.gov.uk. Simon Fowler's well-illustrated *Sources for Labour History* was published by what is now The National Archives in 1995. It provides guidance on official records which relate to trade unions, as well as much other useful data for those interested in the wider labour movement.

Another site for trade-union data, and also material on the membership and income of friendly societies, is the Parliamentary Archives which holds records of both Houses of Parliament, see: http://www.parliament.uk/business/publications/parliamentary-archives/. In the manuscripts division of the National Library of Scotland, George IV Bridge, Edinburgh, there are collections of records of Scottish trades unions, see: https://www.nls.uk/collections/manuscripts and https://www.nls.uk/catalogues/labour-history. There are also many books which may help you in your research, for example, Rodney Mace's *British trade union posters: an illustrated history* (1999). Online there is a description of the contents, which includes 200 posters.

If your ancestor was in a specific trade, you may need to find out where they worked in this trade, when and what precisely they did. This is because they may well have had options as to which union to join. There were different organisations for cordwainers and bootmakers, for example. You can then decide which trade unions the ancestor might have joined. Is there any physical evidence – a membership certificate, a badge or a sash? On badges you might find Paul Martin's *The trade union badge: material culture in action* (2002) of use. There is also a Trade Union Badge Collectors Society, see: https://unionbadges.wordpress.com.

To trace the development of individual unions, a useful source is the six-volume *Historical Directory of Trade Unions* (1980–2009), edited by Arthur Marsh et al. Each entry provides the name of union, the foundation and closure dates and any name changes and amalgamations. There is also information about the membership, leadership and policies and where you can learn more. Copies can be found in The National Archives and in some libraries. Once you have excluded those unions that only operated in times or in places where your ancestor did not live and created a list of the unions whose records you wish to consult, you will need to seek out those records. Many are held in one of the major specialist record offices, although some unions have their own archives. The Royal College of Nursing has institutional records, personal collections, papers, badges, medals and images from the late nineteenth century onwards and some recordings of oral testimony, see: https://www.rcn.org.uk/library/royal-college-of-nursing-archive. The catalogue is at: http://archives.rcn.org.uk/CalmView/default.aspx?&_ga=2.1 7879 5428.1094183949.1520349666-1471810261.1520349666. You can also search for individuals at: http://archives.rcn.org.uk/CalmView/Advanced.aspx?src=CalmView.Persons.

There are also collections in many local council archives, museums and collections. For example, the Jewish Museum London,

Raymond Burton House, 129–31 Albert Street, London NW1 7NB, 020 7284 7384, http://www.jewishmuseum.org.uk/Home, has material relating to Jewish trade unions and a collection of recordings, some of which are of Jewish trade-unionists. It also has materials relating to Jewish friendly societies, including a Ritual Book of the United Jewish Friendly Society. This would have been used at meetings of each lodge of this society. Rosemary Wenzerul's *A Guide to Jewish Genealogy in the United Kingdom* (2008) and her *Tracing your Jewish Ancestors* (2014) both have information about Jewish friendly societies. You may well come across membership cards or admission books, which list who joined the union.

FILM AS A SOURCE

Another source for learning more about your trade-union ancestor is film. In 1924 the Union of Post Office Workers became the first union to use film for promotional purposes. The 40-minute *The UPW Film* showed the early efforts to organise in the late nineteenth century and included footage of post office employees at work. It was intended to show the membership with the roles played by the leadership. The film toured the country for several years and was welcomed by unions and local Labour parties. In 1924 a film was made of a TUC tour of the Soviet Union but it seems to have disappeared. Efforts were also made at local level. In 1935 a group of rank-and-file building workers made a 10-minute film, *Construction*, about the work of builders and a nine-day strike. It was shown around London in 1936. Many of the documentary films of the period feature scenes of people at work. For example, *Shipyard* (1935), a 24-minute film about the construction and launch of a liner, is included on two BFI DVD compilations, see: http://www.screenonline.org.uk/film/id/560369/index.html. An extract featuring workers at the Vickers shipyards in Barrow can be found online at: https://www.youtube.com/watch?v=T2JWvpsU4Qs. The unions were not alone in making films of workers. Although Jill Craigie's *Blue Scar* (1949) is a drama about miners in south Wales and funded by the

National Coal Board, there is a lot of material about trade unions and most of the cast were local amateurs. Craigie was a documentary maker and this film has many elements of documentary about it. It can be seen at: https://free-classic-movies.com/movies-04a/04a-1949-05-01-Blue-Scar/index.php. A collection of films and reviews of them is available via the British Film Institute, BFI, http://www.bfi.org.uk.

The BFI also has what it claims is 'the largest accessible archive of British TV programmes in the world'. If your ancestor appeared in a television programme about his or her fraternal association, you could search for footage here. For example, in 1949 a film was made about the 150th anniversary, in 1948, of the Royal Masonic Institution at Bushey Senior School, Hertfordshire. The film was sponsored by the Royal Masonic Institution for Boys. In 1974 the Ancient Order of Foresters sponsored the production of a film about the Society, *The Friendly People*. In 1969 Westward TV made *The Iddesleigh Men's Friendly Society*. Founded in 1838, it was one of only two such active societies in Devon. There is footage of the 150th Society's Club Day on 1 May. The celebrations included a church service and a parade at which members wore a blue ribbon.

The National Library of Scotland, George IV Bridge, Edinburgh, https://www.nls.uk, collection includes a number of films of trade-unionists. *History of the Tailor and Garment Workers Union* (1951) includes footage of a union conference attended by Labour prime minister Clement Attlee and the co-founder and General Secretary of the Transport and General Workers Union who in 1951 was Foreign Secretary Ernest Bevin. The film features a dramatised account of the foundation of the union. *Scottish Miners Gala Day* (1953), filmed in Edinburgh, features the procession and rally, the Scottish Miners' youth contingent, pipe band and sports competitions. There is also the documentary about industrial relations in the Fairfield's shipyard on the Clyde, *The bowler and the bunnet* (1967), narrated and directed by Sean Connery.

DIGGING DEEPER

There are probably no records of many of the friendly and fraternal associations which existed in the eighteenth and nineteenth century or earlier. Often the material available to us is thin, with nothing recorded about myths, regalia or membership. You may well come across items such as a badge or a single reference to a village society, which are difficult to contextualise and remain mysterious. If you find out new information about your ancestor and the society of which that person was a member, it would be helpful if you shared your information on the web. Other researchers will be grateful and you might meet a fellow enthusiast who can help you. Moreover, you would be continuing a tradition. Although unions, Freemasonry and friendly societies have all developed in different directions from their common ancestors and have not always agreed about the best way forwards, a central reason why Freemasonry, friendly societies and unions have survived is because they have offered communal support in a risky world. They remain part of the same family and need to be understood in context with one another. They have shared and exchanged ideas and learnt from one another. That is a good model for sociable, collaborative, informal, learning and teaching.

BIBLIOGRAPHY

Anderson, Janice. W*orking Life in Britain 1900 to 1950*, London, Time Warner, 2005.
Barnes, George. *Workshop to War Cabinet,* London, Herbert Jenkins, 1924.
Beveridge, William. *The Evidence for Voluntary Action: Being Memoranda by Organisations and Individuals, and Other Material Relevant to Voluntary Action*, London, Allen and Unwin, 1949.
Beveridge, William. *Voluntary Action: A Report on Methods of Social Advance*, London, George Allen & Unwin, 1948.
Bierce, Ambrose. *The Devil's Dictionary,* New York and Washington DC, Neale Publishing, 1911.
Bliss, Mary and Day, Mary. *Cirencester Benefit Society 1890–1990,* Stroud, Alan Sutton, 1990.
Buss, Harold F. and Burnett, R.G. *A goodly fellowship: A History of the Hundred Years of the Methodist Local Preachers Mutual Aid Association 1849–1949,* London, Epworth, 1949.
Calderwood, Paul. *Freemasonry and the Press in the Twentieth Century. A National Newspaper Study of England and Wales,* Farnham and Burlington VT, Ashgate, 2013.
Campbell, Richardson. *Rechabite history; a record of the origin, rise, and progress of the Independent Order of Rechabites, Salford Unity from its institution on August 25th, 1835, to the present time,* Manchester, The Board Of Directors Of The Order, 1911.
Centerprise. *Working Lives Volume Two. Hackney 1945–77*, London, Hackney WEA, 1977.
Clark, Peter. *British clubs and societies 1580–1800: the Origins of an Associational World,* Oxford, Oxford University Press, 2000.
Cooper, Walter G. *The Ancient Order of Foresters Friendly Society, 150 years, 1834–1984,* Southampton, Executive Council of the Ancient Order of Foresters, 1984.
Crail, Mark. *Tracing Your Labour Movement Ancestors: A Guide for Family Historians,* Barnsley, Pen & Sword, 2009.
Dash, Jack. *Good Morning, Brothers!,* London, Lawrence & Wishart, 1969.
Dean, Brenda. *Hot Mettle: SOGAT, Murdoch and me*, London, Politico's, 2007.

Dennis, Mark and Saunders, Nicholas. *Craft and Conflict: Masonic trench art and military memorabilia,* London, Savannah Publications, 2003.

Draffen, George. *Scottish Masonic Records, 1736–1950. A list of all the lodges at home and abroad chartered by the Grand Lodge of Scotland, Lodge Mother Kilwinning, Lodge Melrose St. John with the dates of their charters, places of meeting, alter actions in numbers and colour of clothing,* Perthshire, Coupar-Angus, 1950.

Edwards, Amelia. *A thousand miles up the Nile,* Norwalk, CT, Eastern Press, 1991 (1st edn 1877).

Fisk, Audrey. *Mutual self-help in Southern England 1850–1912,* Southampton, Ancient Order of Foresters' Historic Trust, 2006.

Fisk Audrey and Logan, Roger. *Grandfather was in the Foresters,* Southampton, Ancient Order of Foresters' Historic Trust, 1994.

Fowler, Simon. *Sources for Labour History*, London, Public Record Office, 1995.

Fowler, Simon and Weinbren, Daniel. *Now the War is Over: Britain 1919–1920,* Barnsley, Pen & Sword, 2018.

Fuller, Margaret. *West Country Friendly Societies: An Account of Village Benefit Clubs and their Brass Pole Heads,* Lingfield, Oakwood Press for the University of Reading, 1964.

Gildart, Keith and Howell, David. *Dictionary of Labour Biography, Volume XIV,* Basingstoke, Palgrave Macmillan, 2018 (note other volumes in this series have other editors and publishers).

Gould, Robert Freke. *Concise history of Freemasonry*, London, Gale & Polden, 1904.

Gould, Robert Freke. *The History of Freemasonry: Its Antiquities, Symbols, Constitutions, Customs, Etc.: Embracing an Investigation of the Records of the Organisations of the Fraternity in England, Scotland, Ireland, British Colonies, France, Germany and the United States: Derived from Official Sources*, 3 vols, London, Caxton, 1882–7.

Hamill, John. *The Craft. A history of English Freemasonry*, Leighton Buzzard, Crucible, 1986.

Hannah, Walton. *Darkness visible: a Christian appraisal of Freemasonry,* Chumleigh, Augustine Publishing, 1988.

Harrison, David and Lomax, Fred. *Freemasonry & fraternal societies,* Addlestone, Lewis Masonic, 2015.

Healey, Denis. *The Time of my life,* London, Michael Joseph, 1989.

Hodge, John. *From Workman's Cottage to Windsor Castle*, London, Sampson Low, 1931.

Bibliography

Jackson, Keith. *Beyond the Craft: The Indispensable Guide to Masonic Orders Practised in England and Wales,* 6th edn, Addlestone, Lewis Masonic, 2012.

Kenney, Scott. *Brought to Light: Contemporary Freemasonry, Meaning, and Society,* Waterloo, Canada, Wilfrid Laurier University Press, 2016.

Lane, John. *Masonic Records 1717–1894,* Version 1.0 (<http://www.hrionline.ac.uk/lane>), October 2011, published by HRI Online Publications.

Leeson, Robert. *Strike: a live history: 1887–1971,* London, Allen and Unwin, 1973.

Lepius, Richard. *Discoveries in Egypt, Ethiopia and the Peninsula of Sinai in the years 1842–1845,* London, Richard Bentley, 1852.

Logan, Roger. *An introduction to friendly society records,* Bury, Federation of Family History Societies, 2000.

MacDougall, Ian (compiler and ed.). *A Catalogue of some labour records in Scotland and some Scots records outside Scotland for the Scottish Labour History Society*, Edinburgh, Scottish Labour History Society, 1978.

Mace, Rodney. *British trade union posters: an illustrated history,* Stroud, Alan Sutton, 1999.

MacKenzie, Kenneth. *Royal Masonic Cyclopaedia,* Wellingborough, Aquarian Press, 1877.

Macnulty, W. Kirk. *Freemasonry, symbols, secrets, significance,* London, Thames & Hudson, 2006.

Marland, Hilary. *Medicine and Society in Wakefield and Huddersfield, 1780–1870,* Cambridge, Cambridge University Press, 1987.

Marriott Wulcko, Laurence. *Some Early Friendly Societies in Buckinghamshire,* Chalfont St Peter, The Author, 1951.

Marsh, Arthur and Smethurst, John (eds). *Historical Directory of Trade Unions*, Aldershot, Ashgate, 2006.

Martin, Paul. *The trade union badge: material culture in action,* Aldershot, Ashgate, 2002.

Mendoza, Harry. S*erendipity: Musings on the Precedence of, and Numbers and Names Used by Lodges and Chapters of the United Grand Lodge of England,* Addlestone Surrey, Lewis Masonic, 1994.

Neave, David. *Feasts, Fellowship, and Financial Aid: South Holderness Friendly Societies,* Beverley, Hedon and District Local History Society, 1986.

Neave, David. *Mutual Aid in the Victorian Countryside: Friendly Societies in the Rural East Riding,* Hull, Hull University Press, 1990.

Newman, Aubrey, Hughes, David and Peacock, Don. *Freemasonry in Leicestershire and Rutland. The 'Other' Orders and degrees,* Leicester, Anchor Print, 2012.

Newman, Aubrey, Peacock, Donald and Hughes, David. *A History of the Masonic Province of Leicestershire and Rutland,* Leicester, Anchor Print, 2010.

Önnerfors, Andreas. *Freemasonry: a very short introduction*, Oxford, Oxford University Press, 2017.

Pagnamenta, Peter and Overy, Richard. *All our working lives*, London, BBC Books, 1984.

Pollitt, Harry. *Serving my time: An apprenticeship to politics*, London, Lawrence & Wishart, 1950.

Ravenhill-Johnson, Annie and James, Paula. *The Art and Ideology of the Trade Union Emblem, 1850–1925*, London, Anthem Press, 2013.

Reid, Alastair. *United we stand: a history of Britain's trade unions*, London, Allen Lane, 2004.

Riley, James C. *Sick, Not Dead: The Health of British Workingmen during the Mortality Decline,* Baltimore, MD, Johns Hopkins University Press, 1997.

Roper, Daniel Herbert and Harrison, John. *The First Hundred Years: 1868–1968: the Story of the National Deposit Friendly Society*, Bristol, National Deposit Friendly Society, 1968.

Saddler, Ian. *A mission in life. The History of Liverpool Victoria Friendly Society*, Liverpool, Liverpool Victoria Group, 1997.

Skelley, Jeffrey. *The General Strike*, London, Lawrence & Wishart, 1976.

Snell, Harry. *Men, movements and myself,* London, J.M. Dent & Sons, 1936.

Solt Dennis, Victoria. *Discovering Friendly and Fraternal Societies*, London, Shire, 2005.

Stanley, Jo and Griffiths, Bronwen. *For Love & Shillings. Wandsworth Women's Working Lives*, London, London History Workshop, 1990.

Thorne, Will. *My life's battles*, London, George Newnes, 1926.

Tregoning, David and Cockerell, Hugh Anthony Lewis. *Friends for Life. Friends' Provident Life Office 1832–1882,* London, H. Melland, 1982.

United Grand Lodge of England. *Directory of Lodges and Chapters,* London, United Grand Lodge of England (annual since 1900).

Vindex. *Light Invisible: The Freemasonry Answer to Darkness Visible,* London, Regency Press, 1952.

Waite, Edward (ed.). *A New Encyclopaedia of Freemasonry*, London, William Rider and Son, 1921.

Weedon, W.J. *History of the Lodge of St John No. 1370, 1870–1953*, London, Royal Masonic Benevolent Institution, 1953.

Weinbren, Daniel. *Generating Socialism: Recollections of Life in the Labour Party,* Stroud, Alan Sutton, 1997.

Bibliography

Weinbren, Daniel. *The Oddfellows: 200 Years of Making Friends and Helping People,* Lancaster, Carnegie, 2010.

Wenzerul, Rosemary. *Tracing Your Jewish Ancestors: A Guide for Family Historians,* 2nd edn, Barnsley, Pen & Sword, 2014.

Wenzerul, Rosemary (ed.). *A Guide to Jewish Genealogy in the United Kingdom,* St Albans, Jewish Genealogical Society of Great Britain, 2006.

Zweig, Ferdynand. *The British Worker*, Harmondsworth, Penguin, 1952.

INDEX

Amalgamated Engineering Union 153, 164
Amalgamated Society of Carpenters and Joiners 139
Amalgamated Society of Engineers 138, 139
Amalgamated Society of Woodworkers 140
Ancient Grand Lodge of England (Antients) 41, 50, 57, 60, 79
Ancient Order of Foresters vii, 4, 12, 13, 15, 40, 69, 92, 94, 96, 98, 99, 110, 113, 117, 124, 128, 177
Ancient Order of Shepherds 112
Anti-Gallicans 45
Appleby Old Friendly Society 92
Approved Society 7, 110, 120, 121, 122, 124, 125, 126, 127, 128
Associated Blacksmiths' Forge and Smithy Workers Society 135–6
Association of Professional and Executive Clerical and Computing Staff 169
Association of Women Barristers 86
Attorney General 55

Beamish open-air museum 83
Bell Friendly Society 92
British Federation of International Co-Freemasonry 81
British Steel Smelters' Association 142

Carfin Colliery Friendly Society 9
charity ix, 1, 3, 12, 14, 37, 38, 48, 49, 56, 63, 82, 86, 87, 88, 90, 98, 117, 118, 140

Masonic Trust for Boys and Girls 63
Royal Masonic Benevolent Institution 64
Royal Masonic Hospital 64
Royal Masonic Institute for Boys 63
Royal Masonic Institute for Girls 63
Chartism 51, 90, 107–9, 137, 173
Civil Service Clerical Association 164
Clerk of the Peace 51, 55, 56, 91
Confederation of Health Service Employees 166
Crewe Co-operative Industrial and Friendly Society 118

Economic League 158
Enginemen's Union Fund 92

film and television
  Blue Scar 176
  Construction 176
  History of the Tailor and Garment Workers Union 177
  Made in Dagenham 165
  Scottish Miners Gala Day 177
  Shipyard 176
  The bowler and the bunnet 177
  The Da Vinci Code 50
  The Friendly People 177
  The Iddesleigh Men's Friendly Society 177
  The UPW Film 176
Free Gardeners 28, 71, 128
Freemasonry vii, ix, 1, 2, 5, 6, 8, 10,

184

Index

24, 34, 40, 41, 42, 43, 44, 46, 47, 48–88, 178
Albert Edward Lodge 73
Authors' Lodge 73
Balham Lodge 85
Camellia Thea Lodge 73
Chelsea Lodge 72
Clarence Lodge of Instruction 73
Cornubian Lodge 78
Devonshire Emergency Services Lodge, No. 9613 73
Etruscan Lodge 72
Gilbert Greenall Lodge 66
Grand Lodge des Philadelphes, an irregular French Masonic lodge meeting in London 59
Grand Lodge of Ireland 56, 60, 80, 82, 82
Grand Lodge of Scotland 41, 60, 62, 79
Grand Orient of France 59
Hortus Lodge 72
Le Droit Humain 80, 81
Lodge of Friendship 51
Lodge of Illumination 73
Lodge of Probity 79
Lodge of St John 82
Mark and Rose Croix 78
Navy Lodge 62
Palatine Lodge 14
Philanthropic Lodge 67, 68, 69, 72, 78
Provincial Grand lodges 2, 43, 51, 66, 78, 113
Royal Arch 55, 57, 58, 74
Royal Jubilee Lodge 85
Scientific Lodge 72
Shokotan Karate Lodge 73
Sub Aqua Lodge 73

Sunderland the Sea Captains' Lodge 14, 53, 55, 56, 57, 79, 80, 82, 85
United Grand Lodge, England 31, 39, 41, 51
Friendly Society Medical Association 99
Friendly Society of Operative Iron Moulders 6
Friendly Society of Operative Stonemasons 6
Friendly Society of Women (Spalding) 92
Friendly Union of Mechanics 138
Friends of Peace Friendly Society 95

general strikes 124, 147, 149, 151, 153, 163
Glenfield Female Friendly Society 92
Glorious Revolution 44
Grand Order of Israel Friendly Society 126
Grand Order of Water Rats 14
Graphical, Paper and Media Union 170
Great Western Railway Provident Society 100
guilds 4, 7, 9, 35, 37–40

Hampshire Friendly Society 100, 114
Hermetic Order of the Golden Dawn 75
Highland Society 45
Hiram Abiff 39
Home Office 50
Honourable Fraternity of Antient Masonry 80, 81
Independent Order of Rechabites,

Salford Unity Friendly Society 30, 93, 100, 126, 128, 130
International Order of Good Templars 14
Irish National Foresters 6

Journeymen Steam Engine and Machine Makers Friendly Society (Old Mechanics) 138

Kilmarnock Coal Cutters Society 92
Knight Templars 35, 50, 113

legislation
  1793 Act for the Relief and Encouragement of Friendly Societies 50, 90, 91, 95, 133
  1795 Seditious Meetings Act 50
  1795 Treason Act 50
  1799 Combination Act 51, 53, 133
  1800 Combination Act 51
  1829 Friendly Societies Act 106
  1832 Anatomy Act 104
  1832 Great Reform Act 107
  1834 Poor Law (Amendment) Act 63, 105
  1860 Checkweighman's Act 160
  1871 Trade Union Act 132, 139, 141
  1874 Factory Act 141
  1875 Conspiracy and Protection of Property Act 141
  1875 Employers and Workmen Act 141
  1875 Friendly Societies Act 106
  1906 Trades Dispute Act 144
  1911 National Insurance Act 8, 110, 120, 123
  1911 Shops Act 82
  1914 Defence of the Realm Act 146
  1915 Munitions of War Act 144
  1927 Trades Disputes Act 163
  1946 National Insurance Act 125
  1961 Trustee Investment Act 129
  1970 Equal Pay Act 165
Leicester Bond Street Friendly Society 92
Liverpool Cotton Brokers' Association 72
London Corresponding Society 51

Maidstone Society for Useful Knowledge 45
Markfield Female Friendly Society 110
Mary Gardner's Friendly Society 92
Masonic press 58
Millwrights' Friendly Society 139
Modern Grand Lodge (Moderns) 41, 57, 60
music 44, 45, 67, 93, 104, 164

National Agricultural Labourers' and Rural Workers Union 143, 155
National Amalgamated Approved Society 126
National Association of Local Government Officers 167
National Graphical Association 170
National Health Service 124, 126
National Propaganda 158
National Union of Public Employees 170
newspapers and magazines
  Ars Quatuor Coronatorum 70
  Cheshire Observer and General Advertiser 1
  Co-Mason, 81
  Common Cause 81
  Conveyer 159

Index

Daily Mail 86
Daily Mirror 62, 159
Engineers' Bulletin 159
Ford Worker 163
Foresters' Miscellany 12
Freemasons' Quarterly Review 58, 63
Gavel 81
Guardian 26, 32, 86
Labour History Review 86
Mining Journal 70
New Propeller 159
Northern Star 108, 109
Odd Fellow Magazine 12, 102, 107, 108, 109, 125, 129
Solidarity 159
The Times 25
Trade Union News and Tatler 162
Trades Newspaper and Mechanics Weekly Journal 135
Unknown World 75
Vote 81
Votes for Women 81
Worker 159
Nottinghamshire and District Miners' Industrial Union 157
Nottinghamshire Miners' Association 157

Oddfellows 1, 19, 24, 27, 28, 35, 40, 66, 69, 79, 94, 99, 100, 101, 106, 107, 109, 110, 113, 115, 117, 119, 120, 121, 122, 123, 124, 125, 126, 127, 128, 129, 130, 131
   Independent Order of Oddfellows, Manchester Unity vii, 3, 14, 15
   Nottingham Ancient Imperial Unity of Oddfellows 92
   Nottingham Imperial Oddfellows 14, 110

Nottingham Oddfellows Friendly Society 92, 101
Independent Order of Rechabites, Salford Unity Friendly Society 30, 93, 100, 126, 128, 130
Orange Order 4, 6, 26
Order of the Golden Dawn 75
Order of the Secret Monitor 15, 80
Order of Women Freemasons 80, 81
Organisation for the Maintenance of Supplies 152

Police Mutual Assurance Society 68
political parties
   British Union of Fascists 157
   British Socialist Party 149
   Communist Party 149, 154, 156, 160, 169, 173
   Conservative Party 28, 31, 67, 86, 109, 124, 150, 153, 158, 164, 169, 170
   Labour Party 9, 31, 75, 110, 124, 125, 141, 142, 144, 145, 147, 148, 153, 154, 157, 161, 163, 164, 167, 169, 170, 173, 176
   Liberal Party 28, 31, 67, 110, 124, 140, 141, 144
   Scottish National Party 167
Poor Law 41, 63, 105

Regius Manuscript 40
religion
   Catholic 39, 40, 61, 75
      Pope 3, 61
   Christianity 37, 39, 43, 48, 61, 62
   Hindu 79
   Huguenot 6, 44
   Jews 6, 20, 80, 175, 176

Muslim 79
Parsi 79
Protestant 4, 6, 14, 44, 61, 91
Sikh 79
Romans/Roman period x, 4, 35, 36–39, 61
Royal Academy 45
Royal Antediluvian Order of Buffaloes 14
Royal Berkshire Friendly Society 100
Royal College of Nursing 175
Royal Commissions 61, 41
   1867 Royal Commission on Trade Unions 141
   1872 Royal Commission on Friendly Societies 119, 120
   1874–85 Royal Commission on Labour Laws 141
Royal Foresters 40, 112
Royal St Crispin Society 41
Royal Society of Antiquaries, 45
Royal Society of Edinburgh 45
Russian Revolution 149

Salvation Army 118
Scottish Weavers Association 39
Sheffield Society for Constitutional Information 50
Smiths Benevolent, Sick and Burial Society 138, 139
Society of Artists 45
Society of the Horseman's Word 71
Sons of Temperance 128
South Wales Coal Owners' Association 158
South Wales Miners' Federation 160, 161
Southwark Assurance Friendly Society 95

Town Smarts 45
trades councils 140, 157
   Brent 169
   Islington 168
   Limerick 149
   London 135, 140
   Manchester and Salford Women's 148
Trades Union Congresses 134, 135, 136, 140, 141, 143, 146, 148, 167, 172

Unanimous Club 47
Unison 171
United Irishmen 6, 51
United Machine Workers' Association 157

war 58
   American Civil 54
   Anglo-Afghan 29
   Anglo-Zulu 29
   First World 21, 81, 82, 144, 146, 147
   memorials 60
   Napoleonic 59, 133
   Second World 22, 32, 84, 126, 158, 162, 163
   Seven Years 75
Welsh
   Assembly 85
   clubs 45
   language 6
   nationals 75, 160
West Suffolk Society 100
Women's Friendly Society, Belgrave 92
Women's Police Service 147
Women's Trade Union League 146, 171